Independent Movement and Travel in Blind Children

A Promotion Model

a volume in
Critical Concerns in Blindness

Series Editor:
Ronald J. Ferguson, *Louisiana Tech University*

Volume Editor:
Jeremy T. Miner, *Louisiana Tech University*

Critical Concerns in Blindness Series

A Project of the

Professional Development and
Research Institute on Blindness

The Professional Development and Research Institute on Blindness was established by the Louisiana Center for the Blind in 1999 and became a center at Louisiana Tech University in October 2001. The purpose of the Institute on Blindness is to provide leadership in creating programs and conducting research that recognizes the socially constructed assumptions underpinning the current structure of the blindness system and research being done on blindness. As a result, the Institute on Blindness provides alternative programs and research that expands the boundaries of the blindness field. Currently the Institute on Blindness offers two graduate programs—orientation and mobility and teachers of blind students (often referred to as teachers of the visually impaired).

The mission of the institute is to advance the blindness field by providing the blind and professionals serving the blind with innovative programs and conducting meaningful research that will empower blind people to live independent and productive lives.

Books in the series

*Making It Work: Educating the
Blind/Visually Impaired Student in the Regular School* (2005)
by Carol Castellano

Education and Rehabilitation for Empowerment (2005)
by C. Edwin Vaughan and James H. Omvig
edited by Ronald J. Ferguson

The Blindness Revolution: Jernigan in His Own Words (2005)
by James H. Omvig

Seeing Beyond Blindness (2006)
by Shelley Kinash and Ronald J. Ferguson

*The Blind Need Not Apply: A History of Overcoming Prejudice
in the Orientation and Mobility Profession* (in press)
by Ronald J. Ferguson

Independent Movement and Travel in Blind Children

A Promotion Model

by

Joseph Cutter

INFORMATION AGE
PUBLISHING

Charlotte, North Carolina • www.infoagepub.com

Library of Congress Cataloging-in-Publication Data

Cutter, Joseph.
Independent movement and travel in blind children : a
promotion model / by Joseph Cutter.
    p. cm. — (Critical concerns in blindness)
  Includes bibliographical references.
  ISBN 978-1-59311-603-3 (pbk.) — ISBN 978-1-59311-604-0 (hardcover)
  1. Blind children—Orientation and mobility. 2. Motor ability in
children. I. Title.
  HV1596.5.C88 2007
  362.4'18—dc22
                              2006101884
1-59311-603-9 978-1-59311-603-3 - Paper
1-59311-604-7 978-1-59311-604-0 - hardcover

ISBN 13: 978-1-59311-603-3 (pbk.)
ISBN 13: 978-1-59311-604-0 (hardcover)
ISBN 10:   1-59311-603-9 (pbk.)
ISBN 10:   1-59311-604-7 (hardcover)

Printed in the United States of America

To

My daughter, Melissa Cutter

Who inspired me
to understand the needs of all children,
by filling my life with love, joy, and respect for
how children learn.

And

Blind Children

Who taught me, guided me, and trusted
my involvement with them. May this book
facilitate their journey toward independence.

CONTENTS

CHAPTER

PREFACE

The blind person is not a deficient sighted person.
—Fredric K. Schroeder

What are our beliefs about blindness that fuel and guide our actions with blind children? There are basic questions parents of blind children, professional service providers, and other interested parties in the care of blind children must address if we are to clarify and make positive our relationships and interactions with blind children. Our attitudes and beliefs about blindness, as well as the concepts and practices that we use to guide the blind child's development, will form the foundation to promote independent movement and travel in blind children.

- What do we know about blindness?
- What do we truly believe about how blind children become independent adults?
- Other than the child not seeing or seeing well, what do we believe are the inevitable consequences of blindness?
- What do we believe about the goal, independent movement and travel in blind children, that we are trying to reach?

Independent Movement and Travel in Blind Children: A Promotion Model, pp. ix–xi

- What happens to the belief system in blind children, in their ability to move and travel independently, when we teach them that someone else will take responsibility for their movement by guiding them in a manner that is not age/stage (developmentally) appropriate?
- What do we believe about the parent-child relationship and how it contributes to developing independent movement and travel in blind children?

For the answers to these questions and many others, I invite you to read this book. You may be a parent of a blind child looking for more information to understand your child's movement and travel needs, or a blind person considering mentoring a young blind child. You may be a student interested in the field of orientation and mobility (O&M), an O&M professional or other professional service provider with questions about working with blind children, especially the early intervention and preschool population. Whoever you are and whatever your purpose in reading this book, your point of view about blind children may be nurtured, questioned, or challenged. Whatever the outcome from reading this book, I hope it will stimulate your thinking about the independent movement and travel of blind children.

By reading this book, you will have a part of the continuum of information about the concepts and skills blind children need as they grow in the early years. You place yourself at an advantage being more fully informed, and therefore, will expand the possibilities available to you and the blind children in your care. You have a right and a responsibility to acquire a more complete picture of their movement and travel needs. You may agree or disagree with what is written in these pages. *You have a choice about what to believe about blindness.* It is not an informed choice, however, when you don't have all the available information; instead you have, as a friend of mine has said, "uninformed chance."

I have worked in the field of blindness for more than 35 years as an O&M specialist. My beliefs, attitudes, thinking, and practices working with the blind child have changed over time. It was not the blind child who changed but my *perception* of the blind child that changed. My attitudes and thinking about blindness changed from a deficit-orientation to an asset-orientation. This book is an attempt to present and discuss the positive concepts and practices that promote independent movement and travel in blind children. It is a written testimonial with photographs. The photos are a chronicle to illustrate the tested "recipes for success" offered in this book.

Over the years I have come to know that "knowledge is power and information gold." I value sharing information that is reliable and useful to empower parents, professional service providers and other interested parties. Whatever your interest and whatever your point of view regarding the independent movement and travel of blind children, read on with an open mind and an open heart, for the future of blind children should shine as 24-karat gold.

ACKNOWLEDGMENTS

How can I review a career of more than 3 decades and acknowledge all those persons who have contributed to the development of this book? How can I show appreciation to all the children and their parents who trusted me to address their questions, doubts, fears and desire for a hopeful future? How can I say *thank you* to so many people who contributed to my understanding of blindness and the needs of blind children? I believed that the best way to acknowledge the contribution of so many would be to write this book.

I had the opportunity to be taught by experts. They were the blind children, their parents, and blind adults who afforded me positive role models. They are all my mentors.

I was fortunate to have known the blind children who developed as any typical child and gave me a *positive standard* to raise my bar of expectations for *all* blind children. I have been privileged to also know blind children who were born severely premature, who caused the medical books to be rewritten because of their will to live and learn. Additionally, it was the multiple disabled blind children who taught me, one step at time, to be more accurate with my own understanding of development in all blind children. Parents of deaf-blind children, like Kathy Gabry,

Independent Movement and Travel in Blind Children: A Promotion Model, pp. xiii–xvi

and of multiple disabled blind children, like Linda Zani Thomas, who are the *voice and advocate* for their children, taught me never to forget the importance of the child's personality, no matter what the developmental level of the child may be.

There were the parents who educated me about their day-to-day life with their blind child, sharing with me their insights and loving suggestions. Then there are the parents who organized and formed Parents of Blind Children (POBC) in New Jersey and made Carol Castellano their president. For more than a decade this organization has been a formidable force in facilitating positive changes in policy and practices in the state agency where I worked. Carol Castellano, POBC, and I developed a partnership on behalf of blind children that guided me and made me a better professional. And there were other parent support groups, such as Child Light in Canada that nurtured and shared in my journey toward understanding the needs of blind children.

I am truly grateful to the members of the National Federation of the Blind (NFB) in New Jersey who mentored me in understanding what consumers require for full participation in society. They were Joe Ruffalo, Ever Lee Hairston, Jerry Moreno, David De Notaris, Jerilyn Higgins, and many more. There are those on the national level of the NFB whose teamwork of expertise guided my development, including Barbara Cheadle, president of the National Organization of Parents of Blind Children, and Joanne Wilson, former director of the Louisiana Center for the Blind and former commissioner of Rehabilitation Services for the United States. There is Dr. Fredric K. Schroeder, the former commissioner of Rehabilitation Services for the United States and the first blind O&M professional to give me developmental guidance for working with young blind children. There are many other blind travel instructors, like Arlene Hill, who gave me my first lesson under sleep shades by a blind instructor, and Jeff Altman, who educated me about structured discovery learning.

Dr. Ruby Ryles offered me the first opportunity to teach early childhood orientation and mobility (O&M) to students at Louisiana Tech University who would become O&M professionals and teachers of blind students. And each year these students energize and fuel me.

There were coworkers at the New Jersey Commission for the Blind and Visually Impaired who inspired my interest and guided the development of my early childhood approach. My first supervisor in O&M, Don Carugati, invited me to work with blind children and provided me a positive approach to working with them. And then there's Donna Panaro, a parent of a blind child and an O&M professional, who encouraged me through my emotional low points from dealing with the "system," to be persistent and not compromise my beliefs and practices.

There were the specialists in early childhood development that educated me. For example, the early intervention programs in New Jersey who had never heard of an O&M specialist let me into their doors to observe, learn and assist them in their programming. And Dr. Lorraine McCune, head of the Infant Studies Department of Rutgers University, taught me so positively, conscientiously and thoughtfully about the development of babies.

I also want to extend my appreciative thank you to Dr. Ronald Ferguson of the Professional Development and Research Institute on Blindness, for his understanding and patience regarding deadlines and delays. I owe a debt of gratitude to three reviewers of my book: Carol Castellano, Doris Willoughby, and Mark Riccobono. Their input was vital to reorganizing and reworking the final draft of the book. Likewise, Jeremy Miner, who reviewed the book and assisted me in editing, guided me to "fine tune" the final draft. I would not have been able to be faithful to the intent and purpose of this book without his editorial support.

Many thanks to the parents of the children I worked with over the years and for their permission to take photos that would show their children in a positive light. There were so many photos that I only wish space would have allowed me to include more in this book. My thanks to the Lilliworks Active Learning Foundation, which has graciously given permission to use several photos that were taken at the North American Active Learning Convention in February, 2005.

And finally, thank you to my daughter and friends whose encouragement to continue writing during long cold winter months warmed my heart and fingers so that I could create, type and finish this book.

To these above individuals and others, I owe a debt of gratitude for their time, patience, and support. Their partnership and guidance directed my teaching for positive outcomes. It is my hope that my *thank you* in the form of this book brings a smile to their faces.

INTRODUCTION

All the forces in the world
are not so powerful as an idea whose time has come.

—Victor Hugo

Unlike many books and articles on orientation and mobility (O&M) for blind children, this one is not about the effect of blindness on movement. Such an inquiry is self-defeating from the start, as it often begins with misconceptions and deficit-thinking about blindness and the blind child's early motor development. *Instead, this book is about the effect of movement on development and the importance of movement experiences for the development of independent movement and travel in blind children. It has a clear premise: blind children must become "active movers" if they are to become independent "travelers."*

The time has come for the O&M profession to partner with consumers and the organized blind and promote the independent movement and travel of blind children in a way *that is philosophically sound and utilizes practices that are* "true to the child." Parents, the organized blind, university preparatory programs in O&M, the O&M professional, and other professional service providers must all become participants in promoting a reliable child-centered approach.

The organized blind have offered solutions and partnerships with professional service providers for decades and
have taken steps in a positive direction by advocating for
early use of cane travel, thus promoting the independent
movement and travel of blind children. The National
Organization of Parents of Blind Children, through its
seminars and publications, has promoted a clear, reliable
and useful message regarding independent movement
and travel for children for many years.

As an O&M service provider who has partnered with the
organized blind and professional blindness organizations,
my purpose in writing this book is to create a "Promotion
Model" blueprint that will contribute to our understanding of independent movement and travel in blind children. The goals of this book are:

- To increase knowledge of a developmental, child-
  centered approach that is an alternative to the conventional practices which derive from an adult-centered model;
- To increase confidence on the part of adults in the
  blind child's life in thinking about the child's independent movement and travel needs;
- To facilitate the setting of age/stage appropriate
  movement and travel expectations for blind children;
- To promote in blind children a positive self-perception about their own movement and travel and a
  view of themselves as active movers and independent
  travelers; and
- To provide information that will be a catalyst for positive change in the field of O&M.

Why do I believe these goals will be achieved? Simple:
what is written in this book is solid in its philosophy and
practices because it is developmentally based and derived

from the blind child's "need to know" and "drive to move." It is confidence-based because it has run the gauntlet of consumer testing over the years and has been refined and made ready as a recipe for success. Therefore, if you incorporate the perspectives offered in this book into your own personal knowledge base, you will not be disappointed. This book offers a Promotion Model orientation to O&M, the independent movement and travel needs of blind children. *This means that what matters most is not how much vision children may have, but how many skills of independent movement and travel they possess.*

Several books have influenced my philosophy, developmental perspectives, strategies and practices, resulting in a Promotion Model for blind children. I would highly recommend these books to you to expand your knowledge base regarding independent movement and travel and other skills of blindness. First, *Cognitive Learning Theory and Cane Travel Instruction: A New Paradigm,* by Richard Mettler, provides a comprehensive theoretical explanation of O&M from an alternative, blindness perspective. Second, *Modular Instruction for Independent Travel for Students who are Blind or Visually Impaired: Preschool through High School,* by Doris M. Willoughby and Sharon L. Monthei, offers comprehensive and detailed information about the instruction of cane travel skills. Third, *Early Learning Step by Step: Children with Vision Impairment and Multiple Disabilities,* by Lilli Nielsen, presents an in-depth developmental guide in early childhood development and precise information on early development and intervention. And last but not least, *Making It Work: Educating the Blind/Visually Impaired Student in the Regular School,* by Carol Castellano, puts forward a "how to" regarding successfully developing an educational program for blind and visually impaired students in the regular school. These four books are listed in the Resources section of this book and in my opinion are the best in the field of blindness covering their respective topics.

This book takes a little of the theoretical, instructional, developmental, and "alternative-skill approach" and weaves together this information with the perspectives I have gained in my experiential journey with blind children. Tying these strands together creates a new and unique body of knowledge, the promotion of the independent movement and travel in blind children. This results in the Promotion Model.

Let me tell you a little about how I identify myself as a professional service provider in the field of blindness and about how I describe the population of children discussed in this book. I do not call or consider myself a "vision consultant," a common label for professionals working with blind children. I remember years ago, knocking on the door of a home and the parent came to the door. I introduced myself as a vision consultant. The parent said, "My child does not have eyes to see, and therefore, no vision to consult" and slammed the door in my face. A moment later, she opened the door, apologized for shutting the door so abruptly, and expressed her frustration to me about using the term *vision consultant for blind children.* From that day forward I never used this term again. Instead, I thought about what I really offered to blind children, both totally blind and partially sighted. It was the *blindness skills* that work for all blind children, including those children who are visually impaired and not legally blind. Therefore, I refer to myself as a "blindness consultant."

In addition, I have chosen to describe children as blind and partially sighted rather than "visually impaired" for three reasons.

First, I have met many blind people who prefer to be referred to as blind rather than visually impaired. The word "impaired" implies a deficit and has a negative connotation, whereas the word "blind" represents a characteristic, one among many, that describe a person.

Second, the literature in the field of blindness is *dominated* by the term "visually impaired" and the "B-word" is rarely used. For example, in one early intervention video produced by a program specializing in blind children, a child with only "light perception" is *not* referred to as blind but as "visually impaired." In addition, in many programs and agencies servicing the blind and visually impaired, the visually impaired child is *not* "legally blind." This child usually possesses an amount of vision that does not qualify as legal blindness but does qualify for services. This child may benefit *from* the skills of blindness too, along with the blind/partially sighted (legally blind) child. Therefore, for the purpose of this book, I want to place the emphasis on the "B-word," blind, in a positive light, not to be avoided or thought of as the "description of last resort."

Third, this book does not use a "person-first" language. For example, when describing the blind child, it is often written as the *child who is blind,* placing the word *child* first. This is not a native English expression. In everyday language it is more acceptable to describe the child as a *blind child,* blindness being the adjective and the child the noun. It is interesting to note that in books using person-first language, *the blind child is described as "the child who is blind" and the child with sight as the "sighted child."* Why is it acceptable to describe sight as a characteristic for the sighted child but not blindness as a characteristic for the blind child? The inequality and the view of blindness in a negative light is obvious.

Another factor that influenced the perspectives in this book is that I was trained, as are the majority of O&M specialists, in the conventional approach to O&M, developed by the Veteran's Administration after World War II, as a result of soldiers being blinded while in combat. To understand the divergence of the Promotion Model from this conventional approach, three observations are made about the conventional O&M.

First, it is adult-centered in its philosophy and practices. It promotes precane skills before the learning of the cane. One of these precane skills is called the sighted/human guide. This is the skill used by blind people to follow the lead of another person, usually sighted. In conventional O&M, this learning to use a guide is the first skill the blind person learns for indoor and outdoor travel. Such an approach seemed logical for the newly blinded, who as adults once had vision, had already developed environmental concepts and movement skills and had been independent in travel. The blind child, however, needs to develop orientation concepts and learn to be an active mover and traveler. This is best developed by an early start to cane travel, rather than by spending many months or years learning precane skills. The priority placed on the sighted/human guide and other precane skills and devices do more to delay the process of independent movement and travel than to facilitate it.

Second, the vision loss of the adult was *perceived* as the loss of doing so many skills that required sight, such as having a job, moving about independently, and interacting socially. This created a deficit-thinking about blindness. The nonvisual skills of blindness, to compensate for the loss of these visual skills, were not emphasized; rather, addressing the varying degrees of loss of sight became the priority.

And third, the thinking about the skills of blindness did not significantly factor into the education of blind children. Instead, a "vision first agenda" was emphasized. From such a perspective, because the worst thing to lose was vision, the most important thing to develop would be the partial or residual sight of the blind child. The nonvisual skills of blindness, known to the organized blind, were not promoted. Why? Because the conventional approach, developed by sighted individuals, knew more about sight than about the skills of blindness. In addition, conventional O&M developed without the input from blind individuals who were experts in nonvisual skills.

The Promotion Model offers an alternative perspective rather than the conventional approach. Consequently, I understand that it will be read and reviewed with a critical eye. There are those who may doubt and challenge the philosophy and practices promoted in this book. I will counter such assertions by recording the successes of blind children who have learned O&M as a result of the philosophy and practices outlined in this book. Additionally, the acceptance by consumers of my beliefs and training methods for young blind children, attest to the validity of this model. I am pleased to partner with the organized blind and attend their conferences and seminars where I continue to learn and share information. I invite parents and professional service providers to try these ideas and practices and observe the positive growth in their children and students.

CHAPTER 1

THE PROMOTION MODEL

A deaf-blind child walking in the rain using his cane and umbrella.

Independent Movement and Travel in Blind Children: A Promotion Model, pp. 1–52

Every human being is a problem in search of a solution
—Ashley Montagu

In order to understand how the Promotion Model relates to the development of independent movement and travel, I will first offer an explanation of orientation and mobility (O&M). The Promotion Model is an alternative to the conventional approach of O&M to teach blind children independent movement and travel skills. Conventional O&M is a program for training blind persons to move and travel safely, confidently, effectively, and independently.

The Promotion Model utilizes this definition and expands on it for blind children. The difference between the conventional approach and what is being offered in the Promotion Model is the "what" and "how" we adults (parents of blind children, O&M professionals, other professional service providers, the school, and concerned others) proceed in reaching the goal of O&M. *The goal of O&M is the independent movement and travel in blind children at an age/stage appropriate time so that children develop the perception of themselves as active movers and independent travelers.*

For blind children and their parents, O&M is a way of life. It is a way of knowing and a way of moving, a process of interaction motivated by a wish to know, a drive to "be there" or go "out there" to the world instead of being separate from it. *It is a process toward independence.* Blind children have a sense of order, an ability to organize their experiences and to improve or build on these experiences. From the earliest sensory and motor behavior to the formation of intentional thought and complex problem solving, the drive to want more and to make more out of what reality at any given moment has to offer will be part of the foundation of getting to know and move in the world.

O&M is about the development of independent movement and travel. What we observe through the maturation of the blind child is this developmental process unfolding over time, the child's getting to know and move in the world, on life's terms. Over time, this progression toward maturity and independence becomes more skill oriented. Parents and other educators in the blind child's life are facilitators and interpreters and invite the child into a safe, interesting space where "visiting the world" will take place. We will offer blind children a menu of experiences that will make sense to them. Where visual acuity is absent (or partially so), sensory acuity is still available.

Research has proven that there is an "interconnectedness" to the sensory systems—touch, sound, smell, taste, vision, and spatial—not to mention the joy of moving and the need to know! The human being employs these senses to "get the job done!" It is an *equal opportunity employer* and does not discriminate between the modalities that provide the sensory information. For example, the sense of touch is primary in integrating and relating to all other sensory systems. A significant part of the brain's functioning is designated to the use of the hand. The skin is the largest organ of the body. The blind child is a "sensation of information." Information gathered will be used to compensate and adapt in the process of progressing toward independence.

All humans enter the world dependent on getting their needs met. Movement needs are no exception. When a child learns anything new, there seems to be a pattern: we do it for the child, then with the child, and then allow the child to do it alone. With parental love and guidance, the alternative skills of blindness (nonvisual skills) and tools for success (such as canes, Braille, and low vision aids), blind children will learn a "can do" attitude. We know we can do for blind children, and they are vulnerable to our doing what they can do for themselves. In other words, we often continue to bring the world to them instead of investing our energies into getting them to go out to the world. We must promote blind children going to and getting involved in the world around them.

Blind children, like all children, are more than a sum of their parts. What is essential is not visible to the eye, but more adaptive and compensatory and is driven from the inside. The eye may see but it is the brain that interprets. The eye does not think for itself! Alternative nonvisual skills and the tools that accompany them, as in using the cane, may look different but the results are the same: functionality, enjoyment, having a life! It has been said that "differences aren't deficits" and we must make this message clear to the blind child in what we do and how we do our intervention.

As an O&M instructor, I have observed how blind children adapt when given the proper information, instruction, and tools. For example, take the phenomenon of what is commonly known as echolocation. This is the use of reflected sound to explore and more efficiently move and travel in the world. When we look at blind babies crawling, we can observe that their hands often slap on the kitchen floor. They are doing this not only for play and amusement, but also to utilize the sound feedback from the environment to avoid or go toward objects. They are "looking to hear." The blind child's hands perform extra movements not needed for the motor act of crawling per se. These additional movements are being used for the same purpose that older children or blind adults may use their feet, or better yet, their cane when ambulating to elicit reflected sound.

Being part of this process of development unfolding over time, partnering with parents of blind children, and sharing in their enthusiasm as the child, for the first time, sits, crawls, stands, walks, uses a cane, and learns to explore interesting spaces and places and things, is a joy and pleasure. When adults acknowledge in blind children their creative nature, spirit, and drive to go to the world, we are facilitators in the process of independence for them. Along with the child, when professional service providers share in the love and developmental guidance of the parents of blind children, we creatively adapt and compensate too. And we are reminded once again that what is essential is not visible to the eye.

THE PROMOTION MODEL

The word promote has many meanings: to advance, further, improve, dignify, elevate, support, encourage, and advocate. It is an action verb, which calls on us to act in the best interests for the future of blind children. The Promotion Model is an alternative approach to conventional O&M. The building blocks of the Promotion Model are the principles, developmental perspectives, strategies, and practices and techniques that fuel and facilitate independent movement and travel. Independent movement and travel in blind children is the essence and goal of the Promotion Model.

The goal of the Promotion Model means freedom, hope, and full participation in society for the blind child. The Promotion Model means freedom for the blind child and freedom for the parent. New possibilities for a positive, asset-oriented perspective and developmental approach are created by the Promotion Model. In this model, the parent is the child's first teacher of O&M, and the parent's role must be respected and nurtured by professional service providers.

For blind children, as for all children, the freedom to move, to be self-amused, and experience the joy of movement is fundamental to being human. When exploring and traveling in the world, children have the need and drive to choose where and when to go and to initiate, sustain, monitor, and terminate their own movement. *Independent movement and travel means making decisions, problem solving, and developing good judgment. For blind children this means moving and traveling in the world with the cane at a very early age.*

For parents, independent movement and travel means freedom because children will be learning to take age/stage appropriate responsibility for their own actions. The Promotion Model gives hope to parents, knowing that their child will grow to full capacity and be a full participant in life. Because the parent is the child's first teacher, it has been said, "the mother's lap is the first classroom." For this "classroom," the parent requires developmental guidance from the professional service provider. Useful, reliable and positive partnerships are needed for parents with O&M professionals and other professional service providers who truly understand the blind child's requirements for independent movement and travel.

One requirement is that parents and the O&M professional both place a high value on early movement and travel. In the Promotion Model, the sighted/human guide technique, where the child holds on to someone else's arm, takes a *back seat* to the blind child's movement. Instead, we encourage children to take age/stage appropriate responsibility for their independent movement and travel by developing self-monitored movement with the cane, which will take a *front seat* on the road to independence.

For the O&M professional, independent movement and travel means offering a developmental menu that respects the alternative skills of blindness. Regarding the partially sighted blind child, professional service providers must use caution not to push vision to the point of inefficiency. This can happen when partially sighted (legally blind) children are not taught the skills of blindness and yet are expected to compete with their sighted peers with only 10% or less of typical vision.

Touch and hearing will be the blind child's most important senses in learning nonvisual skills. Such skills will be the blind child's passport to freedom. Cane travel is a very important life skill for the blind child. *The Promotion Model acknowledges that the use of the cane is part of the readiness for travel.* Readiness serves the goal of independence. In the Promotion Model there is no room for a readiness curriculum that is forever getting the child ready to use the cane with unnecessary tasks that may serve the "curriculum checklist" but not the goal of age/stage appropriate independence in movement and travel. Therefore, the Promotion Model values the early start to cane travel in blind children.

Informed Choice

One of the best ways to treat parents with respect and promote independent movement and travel in blind children is to *offer "informed choice"* as a professional service provider. This means respecting blindness, the skills of blindness, and the parent as the child's first teacher for O&M. To do this, professional service providers must be knowledgeable about the spectrum of conventional and alternative O&M practices. When O&M professionals do not understand or are not "up on" the benefits of a very early start to cane travel, then they are usually "down on it."

O&M professionals must be knowledgeable about the effect the characteristics of the cane have on its use by the child. For example, the length of the cane has a direct effect on the success of the child to navigate safely and effectively. The longer cane approach and the lighter cane approach to travel offer advantages to the traveler over the shorter and heavier cane approach (discussed in chapter 4). By understanding how the characteristics of the cane can have an effect on the blind child's travel, professional service providers can offer such possibilities for more positive experiences in movement and travel.

When professional service providers are not knowledgeable about the conventional and nonconventional approaches to independent movement and travel for children, parents are not benefiting from informed choice. Instead, we are taking a *risk* with the decisions parents will need and want to make for their child and for the blind child's future in independent movement and travel.

Sighted Bias

The Promotion Model acknowledges that there is a "sighted bias" to conventional approaches to O&M. For example, formalized O&M developed after World War II and was created by sighted individuals for blind persons who once had vision. Obviously, none of the veterans who lost their vision during the war were born blind. Therefore, the protocols and content of the curriculum did not have the congenitally blind child in mind. The protocols for teaching O&M practices called for "visual monitoring" of the blind person. This meant that the O&M professional must have vision to observe the blind student in the lesson. We know today that blind people can be and are O&M professionals as well.

As a conventionally trained, sighted O&M professional service provider, I have come to understand how my vision has affected my interactions with blind children. My sighted orientation to the world does not employ all the same skills as a blind person's orientation to the world. There are nonvisual skills that I do not use.

What often results from not employing or not knowing about the skills of blindness is that children will be vulnerable to adults placing low expectations on them, often using misconceptions about blindness to guide their practices. Consequently, the child will experience delays in the acquisition of life skills for independent movement and travel.

Adults have a choice of what to believe about blindness and what information to use to guide their interactions with blind children. We *can* offer developmentally appropriate skills. Whether the child is developing as a typical child or with developmental delays, we can facilitate independence in O&M or interfere with the learning of such necessary skills. Blind children with multiple disabilities are even more vulnerable to being misunderstood. The misconceptions about blind children that guide their educational plan are often the result of lowered expectations for what they can achieve.

Through the organized blind I have learned more thoroughly about the skills of blindness and a blindness perspective that, in functional O&M terms, is at times, different than my sighted perspective. As I have become more educated to an alternate orientation to skill development, I have learned to be more aware of my sighted bias. Over the years, this has made me a more effective instructor, the results of which are demonstrated by the increased success of my students.

Mentoring

In addition to the partnership between the parent and the O&M professional we can add a positive, skilled blind role model for the blind child. One description of a skilled blind role model is a mentor. For example, in the first years of the blind child's development, such a blind adult will have a significant, positive, and hopeful influence on expectations of the child's parents. As the child matures, the mentor's guidance will contribute to positive self-esteem and a "can do" attitude. Parents and professional service providers will find a rich resource for skilled blind mentors among the organized blind who value independent movement and travel in blind children. In the Resources section such organizations are listed.

THE BUILDING BLOCKS
OF THE PROMOTION MODEL

Below are the building blocks of the Promotion Model: First, the philosophy, which is its essence and spirit. Second, the principles, which are the foundational truths that support it. Third, the developmental perspectives, which are the fundamental beliefs to fuel and guide it. Fourth, the strategies, which put the philosophy, principles, and developmental perspectives into a plan for action. And fifth, the practices and techniques, which facilitate and put the strategies into action in the everyday learning and development of life skills for the independent movement and travel of blind children.

THE PHILOSOPHY

Philosophically, we must acknowledge that child development is built on gain and not loss. The adult-centered approach of conventional O&M gives significant consideration to the "loss" of vision that adults experience later in life when they lose vision. When looking at child development, however, the Promotion Model recognizes that loss of vision does not factor in significantly in the developmental gains that children make every day. Children born blind or who lose vision in the first years of life do not experience the type of loss associated with adults who lose vision. These children have not acquired years of developing visual skills or possess a visual orientation to the world that has a long-standing integration into their personality.

For blind children, success is not measured by how much vision they have, but rather is built on how many skills are developed for independent movement and travel. With one skill built upon another, the goal of development is mastery over the environment to move and travel safely, confidently, and independently.

In the Promotion Model, the child leads the way, and if we are willing to learn from the child, many possibilities emerge. As an O&M professional service provider, I have connected with parents of blind children, incorporated them into my service delivery plan and learned much from their experiences with their blind children. I have partnered with the organized blind that have provided me with positive, skilled blind role models for independent movement and travel. The building blocks of the Promotion Model have been developed from years of such learning from blind children, their parents and skilled blind adults (the organized blind). Together, they form the fabric of the "nature and nurture" of independent movement and travel. Together, they present a formidable, alternative program of O&M to promote the independent movement and travel of blind children.

Bottom-Up

The child is not born with concepts of the world. The baby is born with sensory systems, like "fingers of the brain," that gather information. With sensory and motor experiences the child matures over time and gives purposeful thought to what is experienced. One way to describe this process is "bottom-up," which can be described as this—*out of the experience comes the concept.* If the experiences we give blind children are developmentally sound they will experience independent movement and travel age/stage appropriately. Blind children will develop the concept or self-perception of themselves as travelers.

Historically, conventional O&M was developed as an adult-centered approach. Its protocols were developed from an adult point of view for adult learners. For instance, the adult was given the concept of a new skill and the skill demonstrated. Then the newly blinded adult would perform the skill. This can be described as a "top-down" approach, which means that *out of the concept comes the experience*. This is a very different approach than bottom-up, which is the perspective of the Promotion Model.

Bottom-up is driven by the sensory and motor experiences of the child, and top-down driven by the cognitive concepts directing the movements of the adult. For example, when blind children under 3 years of age are learning to use the cane, they will need to be amused, explore, and have fun with their cane. Their movements will be more exaggerated and less refined. On the other hand, these are not the behaviors or the goal of the adult learning cane travel for the first time; adults will be ready to be perform at a different cognitive level of understanding.

When promoting independent movement and travel in blind children we need to approach skill acquisition from the bottom-up, making sure our intervention and practice is suited to the developmental ability of the child. Imposing a top-down approach at a developmentally inappropriate level will meet with frustration and disappointment for both the child and the teacher. As a result, the conventional O&M instructor often assesses that the child is not *ready* for O&M instruction or ready for using a cane. In the latter case a precane device is often used. Within the Promotion Model, however, the blind child *is* ready for instruction, just not from the top-down but rather from the bottom-up.

Differences Aren't Deficits

When learning about the diversity in the infant's capabilities to learn to adapt and compensate, it became easy to understand the different ways blind children learn. Reading Braille or using a cane may look different but is hardly a deficit; instead, it is an asset. *The Promotion Model is an asset orientation to blindness.* For example, historically, in conventional O&M, the use of the cane, particularly for the partially sighted blind child, has often been perceived as a negative. The conventional approach typically views the cane as making the child dependent on its use. Therefore, for many years the cane was viewed as a tool of "last resort." This attitude is slowly changing. *If you view the difference of blindness as a deficit, then you will view the skills of blindness in the same negative light and the child will come to know it. But if you view blindness with a positive attitude, then the child will view the skills of blindness positively also.*

The Responsibility for Travel is the Child's

Blind children learn to be responsible for their own travel when they have the opportunity to learn the necessary skills, as any child needs to learn. They must have opportunity for adequate and appropriate instruction, as well as practice in learning the skills. Some skills the blind child will learn are different from sighted children. These will be nonvisual. As blind children develop their alternative skills, they will learn an age/stage appropriate responsibility for their travel. This means that blind children will be able to self-monitor their own movement, practice independent movement, and travel skills, and like all children, have the opportunity to develop good judgment about the decisions they will need to make to travel in the world.

The in-the-arms baby moves to the floor, then upright and out the door! The blind child needs to be monitored as any child would at a very young age. All too often, when walking in the company of an adult, the blind child's hand is being held far beyond the age of sighted peers. And all too often, as the children get older, they are walking on the arm of another person, as their general way of movement and travel. When someone else is taking responsibility for the blind child's movement, it's time to take a look at what blindness skills are needed to be age/stage appropriate and to take responsibility for independent movement. It is *our* responsibility as adults to facilitate independent movement and travel in blind children. In this way blind children, like sighted children, can take age/stage appropriate responsibility for their own travel.

THE PRINCIPLES

Observation is What is Essential

What is essential is not visible to the eye. Children *observe* the world and their movement in the world through their sensory systems. Sighted children primarily use vision and sound to look, or scan, for spatial orientation, and to observe others and themselves when moving. Instead of sight, totally blind children primarily use touch and sound to "look," or scan, for spatial orientation, and to observe others and themselves when moving. Partially sighted children may use vision to observe for some tasks and non-visual senses for other tasks. The deaf-blind child who is totally deaf and totally blind will use primarily touch. The difference between the sighted and the blind is the senses they use to observe.

The key point about observation: what ultimately matters most is not how much vision or hearing children have but how they can *feel and interpret* their own movement. *The eyes may see but they do not think. Our brains think, interpret sensory information and cognitively plan a response.* We know, for example, that in cortically blind children their eyes may appear to "look," but their brain does not interpret what is seen. The brain is not connected properly to sight. Therefore, they are functionally blind.

So how does the blind child observe? The answer: non-visually, through primarily the use of other sensory information. Our touch is our most important integrating sense. We humans have a sort of "body's eye on itself," the tactile (touch) system on and under our skin. We can tell our position in space at any given moment, where we are going and how to coordinate our movements to get there, all by using our tactile system. *Blind children, like all children, learn best about their movement through their own self-monitored movement.*

With this perspective you can understand the effect on blind children's ability to observe if they are experiencing movement primarily on the arm of another person. When they do so, they will *observe* someone else's movement and not their own. They will expertly learn the skill of how to be guided but not develop an age/stage appropriate self-guiding of their own independent movement and travel.

Learning independent movement and travel is about observation and options. We adults want to increase the options for blind children to move and travel independently. Children can do this best by starting with the early learning of cane travel for age/stage appropriate independence in movement and travel.

Vision is Not a Requirement for Independent Movement and Travel; It is Not a Requirement for Life

Congenitally, totally blind children are evidence that vision is not a requirement for independent movement and travel. They are able to explore the world by using their other sensory systems. Given the opportunity to learn the skills of blindness, these children will develop into independent adults without the use of vision. If children have vision, then they will use it in a natural way. Often, however, "vision stimulation" and training activities result in children using their vision in an unnatural way.

For example, partially sighted children will be taught to look first and then reach with their hand. While this is the natural sequence for sighted children, for children with partial sight or residual vision it is not efficient to visually reach first. The *natural* sequence will be to search for an object first with the hand, pick it up and then perhaps look at it with the eye. Children will tend to use vision to the point that it is useful. In addition, children with partial sight or residual vision are vulnerable to not developing their sensory skills of touch and sound if this type of "vision first" agenda is applied.

If you believe vision is a requirement for independence in movement and travel in blind and partially sighted children, then this assumption will undermine your confidence in their capabilities. Children will sense the doubt and their self-esteem will suffer. If blindness, the lack of sight, totally or partially is seen as a "problem," then where does it leave you? The answer is at a "dead end." Blindness cannot be fixed. If we view, however, that the solution is the child learning an alternative skill to do the task, then we can work toward a realistic, positive goal. We raise the level of expectations, and in so doing, raise the level of the child's performance and self-esteem.

Importance of Preview

Everyone needs preview of what's ahead. Sighted people usually see what's ahead and plan for it. Blind children need to plan for what's ahead too. When moving, no one likes to be startled by confronting an object or another person unexpectedly. This could result in trips and falls or bumps and bruises. Such unsafe and unpleasant encounters will be reduced by the sighted child by using vision and by the blind child by using alternative, nonvisual information. For blind children, the distance sense that is used for preview is sound. In "near space" it is touch. First they touch with their hands and feet, and then as the children develop they rely more on sound beyond arm's reach. When children begin to walk, preview of what's ahead can be received, information gathered, and a plan developed to move safely and effectively by using the cane.

The cane will be the blind child's most valuable tool for acquiring preview throughout life. It will facilitate safe, confident, and effective movement and travel. The cane will provide the blind child with information about what's ahead in the environment. For example, by sliding and tapping the cane side to side, the child will learn about the ground surface ahead and any drop-off that may be coming up. Through experience, the child will learn how to use this information acquired by touch and sound, just like the sighted child learns to use information acquired by vision and sound. The better the quality of the preview, the better the child will be able to plan independent movement and travel. Partially sighted children are vulnerable to having reduced quality of visual preview. The alternative skills of blindness will be needed to give them reliable, quality preview.

The Child Has a Need to Know and Drive to Move

All children need information and have a drive to move and travel in the world. Moving, exploring, questioning and gathering information are all part of a natural process toward independence. If blind children do not get enough information or learn to effectively gather information, then there will be delays in their purposeful thought and movement. As adults, we can stimulate and meet the blind child's need for information and facilitate their drive to move to gather that information. Children first explore their body, then reach out to the people and objects around them, and then move about and visit the world. With the alternative skills of blindness that will be discussed we can offer the child experiences that will be a most natural part of the process of growing, learning, and becoming independent.

For example, once I was working with a kindergarten child on finding her coat hook in one of those old-fashioned coatrooms. She asked me where a particular boy's hook was located and I told her. She scanned with her hands down to his hook and back to her hook and repeated this process several times to make sure she had it right. I asked her why it was so important to find *his* hook and she said, "Because he's my boyfriend." And I said to myself, "Now that's the need to know and the drive to move!"

Blindness is Not a Cognitive Disability

Blindness is a physical disability, a sensory impairment. It is a characteristic of a person. *Blind children are not unique in how they think or how they process information.* They do not think differently than sighted children. The blind child's brain is whole and complete without sight. What will be different is that blind children will employ non-visual skills to compensate for their physical (sensory) disability. How fast or slow they will learn is no different than how fast or slow sighted children will learn. Skill acquisition is more a function of having the opportunity to learn with appropriate instruction and practice.

The Goal is Active Movement

One way to describe the essence of active movement is when children are free to move when and where they want. We want blind children to have the same freedom of choice to move as sighted children. This can be done when children monitor their own movement. Monitoring their own movement occurs when children decide when and where to move and when to start and stop their own movement. When the purposeful thought for movement comes from the child, this is one way to describe "active movement." And when we do the movement for children by manipulating their body, this is one way to describe "passive movement."

Blind children are vulnerable to experiencing more than their share of passive movement. For example, when blind children are manipulated manually by adults, what they experience is passive movement and not their own active movement. This is not the way to learn about the world. We want blind children to view themselves as active movers and independent travelers. Such a self-perception is more likely to occur when they are using a cane to move and travel.

One excellent educational approach that has a positive outcome in active movement for the multiple disabled child has been created by Dr. Lilli Nielsen from Denmark. Her educational approach, called Active Learning, is composed of specifically designed materials to facilitate the learning. Active Learning philosophy, strategies, practices, techniques, and materials are designed to be used by multiple disabled blind children who are primarily functioning under the developmental age of 36 months. Some of

Dr. Nielsen's educational materials and educational methods can be used for typically developing blind children under 3 years of age as well.

One of the main strategies of Active Learning is the "hands off" the child approach. In conventional O&M the blind child is often guided with either a "hands on" approach by adults who teach them or a less invasive approach whereby the blind child's hand rests on the adult's hand to observe the movement. In Active Learning, however, the adult's hands are not guiding or contacting the multiple disabled blind child's hands. Dr. Nielsen believes that these children, functioning below 36 months, do not understand the involvement of the adult's hands. Therefore, they become frustrated and less cooperative because they have not invited the adult to touch and interact with their hands.

Active Learning brings a spotlight of attention on how we do our intervention with multiple disabled blind children, and the typically developing blind child as well. We need to be more thoughtful about our interaction and handling of the body of the blind child and understand the potential obtrusive nature of this manipulation.

Further discussion of Active Learning and how it can relate to the independent movement and travel of blind children is presented in chapter 3 and the Resources section, and photos with descriptions of some of these materials are presented in chapter 5.

Age/Stage Appropriate Behavior is Possible

Blind children do develop age/stage appropriate behavior. This can happen, as it would with any child, if it is expected of the child. *Blindness should never be the reason or excuse not to learn an age/stage appropriate skill.* The reason for not learning in an age/stage appropriate manner is usually the result of lowered expectations, lack of opportunity to learn, lack of practice, or an additional developmental disability that impacts the child's ability to learn. *Whatever the reason for a delay in age/stage appropriate behavior in blind children, it is not blindness. If you make blindness the reason, then you are at a dead end with no other solution. The solution is built on the alternative skills of blindness.* There is always a solution. The skills of blindness raise expectations of adults for blind children. Blaming blindness lowers expectations and, as a blind friend of mine says, "no one aspires to low expectations."

In typical development there is a chronological match between the age of the child and the stage (developmental level) of the child. For example, a child will learn to walk around a year of age, give or take a few months, and this would be considered age/stage appropriate. When there are greater delays outside the "norm," the child may be said to have a developmental delay. For instance, when the child is 2 years old and not walking, such behavior would be considered a delay in development. When this occurs there is a greater, atypical disparity between the child's chronological age and the stage (developmental level) at which the child is functioning.

Blind children may be delayed in development for a variety of reasons that have nothing to do with blindness, just as sighted children may have delays that have nothing to do with sight. Our interventions for these children need to be targeted at the cause of the delay at a specific stage (developmental level).

To continue with the walking example, the child who is 2 years of age but whose stage (developmental level) is 1 year, needs a stage appropriate intervention to learn to walk. Therefore, just as a physical therapist would need to address a delay in walking for the sighted child, the therapist needs to address a delay for walking for the blind child. Just as sight would not be the cause for the sighted child's need for therapy, blindness would not be the cause for the blind child's need for therapy. The therapist is more likely to know about how to work with the sighted child than to work with the blind child. This opens the door where a variety of misconceptions about blindness can misguide the therapist in the "what" and "how" of interventions chosen for the blind child.

As adults in charge of the child's care, we must first "do no harm." We must understand and be able to plan for reliable interventions that are targeted for age/stage appropriate behavior. We must have a realistic standard and practices for age/stage appropriate behavior in the blind child that follow the typical developmental guidelines for all children. Given the appropriate and adequate instruction for the blind child, we will facilitate the acquisition of age/stage appropriate behavior.

The Missing Component(s) of Movement Causes a Delay in Motor Development

We know that blindness in itself does not cause a motor component to be missing because there are blind children who did not miss any motor milestones or components of movement in their development. So when we interact with a blind child who has a delay in motor development we must not have the misconception that the delay is caused by blindness. Such thinking will cause us to get stuck in what we perceive as the problem instead of moving forward with an alternative approach to facilitate the component of movement that is missing and needs to be developed.

Much information has been published about the motor development of blind children that depicts blindness as the cause of motor delays. For example, I took a workshop once with the title: "The Effects of Blindness on Movement." It came to the conclusion that blindness negatively affected the motor development of blind children in the first 3 years of life. Since this was not my experience with or perspective of blindness, I decided to give a workshop on the same subject matter but titled it: "The Effects of Movement on the Development of Blind Children." In the workshop I chose to review the importance of movement on the development of blind children ages birth to 3 and how to facilitate the blind child's motor development during these years.

How we approach a problem will have a great deal to do with the solutions we offer. If blind children are delayed in developing a component of movement, for example, sitting, then we need to work on activities and nonvisual skills that will facilitate sitting. This then is a realistic and workable goal. Viewing blindness as the cause of the delay does not focus us on the real issue and therefore is not a realistic goal.

Tool Usage Sets the Stage for Independence

Fundamental to the history of the human evolution is the use of tools. The tool is usually a hand-held instrument that facilitates getting a job done. For children, toys are their tools. As they learn to manipulate and play with objects, they learn to be proficient in handling tools for their own personal enjoyment, to meet their needs, and to become skilled at mastering their environment. Babies first explore objects in their mouths and then gradually explore objects more in their hands. Then they use objects to reach off body into the world.

There will be no other tool as important to blind children in their development of independent movement and travel than the cane. The cane is a hand-held tool that will facilitate being a traveler in the world like no other tool can. Therefore, it is important that we nurture the development of blind children to develop the progression of tool usage as all children. For blind children, their hands are the perceptual *window* onto the world and the cane will be the main tool they will use to travel in it.

DEVELOPMENTAL PERSPECTIVES

Holistic Nature of the Child

Children are more than the sum of their parts. Like sighted babies, blind babies perceive changes in the environment and respond to those changes. Babies do not know, for example, they are seeing, hearing or touching. The baby is just experiencing! We *specialists* divide the child up to do our specialty. One therapist may specialize in fine motor skills, another in gross motor skills, and still another in speech abnormalities. And, of course, there is the vision specialist. The child, however, is a *generalist*, learning to use all the sensory systems together to make sense out of the world. When we respect the interconnectedness of the sensory systems and how the baby learns, we come to offer a more holistic approach.

Therefore, blind children are much more than children who cannot see or see well. They are creative and curious, willing and able to learn and adapt. They are whole and complete. With our positive guidance and teaching, blind children have a right to grow and develop with all the opportunities to learn that are afforded to sighted children.

Developmental Progressions in the Child

Like all children, blind children go through progressions in development. Such development will be expressed in children's behavior, influenced by the kinds of interaction they will have with their parents and professional service providers. The Promotion Model is particularly concerned with development in early movement milestones—motor development to sit, stand, and walk; transition movements from one motor milestone to another; self-initiated movement; getting connected on body and reaching off body; and orientation to the environment and travel skills. *Parents and professionals must offer a menu of experiences and activities in nonvisual skills that will facilitate this development. In this way blind children will have an early start to the equality, opportunity and security they deserve.*

Because development is accumulative and progressive, the child is less likely to become delayed if we are aware of what we can do at each stage to facilitate the acquisition of skills appropriate to achieving a specific milestone. *This calls on us adults to create an alternative menu of nonvisual skills that parallel the developmental progressions in the child.*

Use "Normal" Child Development as Your Guide

Blind children will develop in the same progressions as sighted children do in their physical, motor, cognitive, emotional, and social development. Except for visual development, the typical development of the blind child follows the typical development of the sighted child. For the partially sighted child, visual development will progress to the point of efficiency in a natural manner.

There is a great variation in human development for the sighted child and we should respect this variation in the blind children's development as well. Despite these variations, children develop along a typical timeline progression. Therefore, when using developmental guides it is imperative that we have guidelines from "normal" child development for the blind child. In this way we will know whether the blind child is on target or behind for typical development. By doing so we will more quickly identify a delay in developing a particular skill and the appropriate alternative skill can be used to facilitate what needs to be learned.

I am not suggesting that blind children will not need specific guidelines in their development for learning non-visual skills. This book offers such information and guid-ance in the area of independent movement and travel skills. *I am suggesting that to use a basic developmental guide for the blind child that is not built on typical child development is to set the blind child apart from sighted peers. This setting apart misguides us into lowering our expectations for the blind child.* We have the responsibility to know and teach alternative skills so blind children can compete on terms of equality with sighted children. Start with normal development as your guide.

Touch is the Integrating Sense

The brain does not discriminate against how it receives information. It just needs input. When the brain gets enough information it can organize and integrate it. "Sen-sory integration" is what we do with sensory information. Blind children are vulnerable to not getting enough input if they are not moving in the world and "taking it all in." Does the brain know it doesn't see? Who knows! What's important is that it doesn't seem to matter. The brain can get the job done with other sensory input than visual.

Touch is of obvious importance to the blind child. If we think of the "fingers of the brain" as our hand, touch is the thumb because it connects best to all the other fingers (senses). *Touch is the sense that integrates and gives meaning to all other sensory information in a way that no other sensory modality can give.* Touch is the number one sense used by the blind. The brain employs the use of touch in a proactive, useful manner to get to know the world.

So much has been written about sight that it would seem that humans can not live without their sight. In a study by the Center for Disease Control and Prevention in the United States, blindness was considered the third most dreaded "disease," after cancer and AIDS. The fact is that we can do without sight, but not without our sense of touch. Many years ago a study was done of babies in institutions, left abandoned by the death of their parents as casualties of war. These babies had intact sensory systems. It was found that those babies who could be held, touched, and nurtured survived and those who could not be given touch affections withered away and died. The results of this study demonstrated that touch was *the* basic essential sensory system that is vital to the survival of all humans more than any other sense.

As a sighted individual, my sight is very important to me, as I have learned to live in the world as a sighted person. If I were forced, however, to give up my sense of vision or touch, I would give up my sense of vision, for I could never survive without touch, but I could survive without vision. And more importantly, I could learn to have a full and satisfying life. We need to acknowledge the primacy of touch for human existence and especially for the lives of blind children. The experiences we give blind children to guide their development should be rich in touch. All too often the partially sighted child is given an overemphasis on visual experiences and the totally blind child on auditory information, as in verbal descriptions of how to do things. Blind children need to touch and to use all their sensory systems. *Let the child's brain decide what it needs or it doesn't need. It is an equal opportunity employer.*

Importance of Play

For children, *work is their play.* The blind child does work best through the process of self-directed play. Children who are curious and organized in their play are likely to be that way in school. Play develops interest, curiosity, and contributes to personality development. Blind children are vulnerable to having their play restricted by adults who *overoccupy their space and time.* The blind child's drive to move and explore will also be restricted.

Dr. Lorraine McCune, head of the Department of Infant Studies at Rutgers University, New Jersey, states: "when play is defined to include all of a baby's freely chosen encounters with objects, a large proportion of the child's waking time is play time." Therefore, if playtime is restricted, blind children do not develop enough of the experiences and practice of freely choosing what interests them. When blind children are restricted in the kind and amount of play they may be allowed to perform, when they are limited by others who are often manipulating them, the context of their understanding of people, places and things will also be limited. Such restrictions and limitations will affect their ability to reason, develop good judgment, and express their true potential.

Independent Movement and Travel is a Confidence-Based Skill

Blind children will have a confidence base to their skills if what they are learning is true to who they are. Learning the nonvisual skills appropriate to blindness builds confidence in how children use their senses and the information they gather for independent movement and travel. Many blind children have received hours upon hours of instruction in O&M and yet lack confidence in their travel. Could it be that what and how they were taught does not build confidence and skill proficiency to travel independently?

Because adequate services in O&M are scarce and often difficult to acquire for the blind child, it stands to reason that the practices that offer the most efficient outcomes for independent movement and travel should be highly valued. O&M must be a confidence-based skill if the child is to be safe, efficient and comfortable in movement and travel. *When children develop a confidence base to their blindness skills, such confidence will last a lifetime.*

Functionality and Dysfunction is the Way the Child is Perceived

Functionality is the philosophy of a program in Hungary that is responsible for educating cognitively and physically disabled children. If we believe the blind child can be functional this perception then raises our expectations. From the child's perspective it is natural to be who they are. It is natural to organize space, use the cane, and move about the world as a blind person. *From the point of view of blind children, they are not dysfunctional and it is the most natural state of being to be blind.* This is also true of the developmentally delayed blind child.

If we believe that the child is dysfunctional because of blindness, we lower our expectations for the child. Much information regarding the development of blind children has been written from a dysfunctional point of view, discussing the *perceived* deficits and restrictions of blindness on the development of the child. The Promotion Model embraces the functionality of the child and builds from there.

STRATEGIES

The Parent is the Blind Child's First Orientation and Mobility Teacher

Parents are in the position to know their child the best and are an excellent resource to professional service providers. In the early years the *parent and child are "one unit" and should be treated accordingly.* When O&M professionals share information with and train parents in independent movement and travel skills, they are respecting this parent-child unit. This creates a formidable partnership that benefits the blind child. It facilitates the learning of independent movement and travel, at home and school. When the parent and the O&M professional are on the "same page," the school is more likely to agree upon the goals for the blind child.

When given the appropriate information, parents can facilitate the developmental progressions in their blind child along with the professional service provider. For example, parents will be able to nurture the motor development of their child to push up from the floor, to sit, stand, and walk. The parent will be the child's first cane travel teacher. Parents will be able to advocate for independent movement and travel for their child in early intervention, preschool, and school. Chapters 2, 3, 4, and 5 give examples of "teaching" practices and techniques for parents to facilitate the development of their child.

Parents are in a position to practice the independent movement and travel skills in a variety of everyday settings with their child. When parents are included as part of the O&M team and as the child's first O&M teacher, their child is more likely to achieve age/stage appropriate behavior in independent movement and travel. The parent as teacher is an excellent opportunity to become involved in the child's development. For example, a father and mother can take turns going on a "cane walk" with the child. This gives parents an opportunity to have "special time" and be involved with the education of their child in a practical, life skill oriented way. It is important that fathers become involved with the education of the blind child along with the mother. The parent as the child's first teacher is a shared experience between mothers and fathers.

Familiarization Before Orientation

Another strategy that can be nurtured in early child development is "familiarization before orientation." Sensory experiences become familiar to the child and eventually lead to thinking about those experiences. Working concepts of orientation make use of those experiences. This process results in the purposeful thought and movement of the child. We can conceptualize familiarization before orientation as a natural, bottom-up strategy the child uses to understand people, things, and places.

First, children explore their own body to become familiar with the body parts and how to use them meaningfully and purposefully. Second, they explore reaching from the body to the environment, the world of objects. Third, children explore spaces and as they become familiar with the characteristics of those spaces, a concept develops of a particular space as a place to visit. We can facilitate this process and natural strategy with practices and techniques that promote these progressions in the development of the child.

For example, before children can use their hands meaningfully, they must discover and experiment with the hands at the midline of the body (chest area of the body). Chapter 2 offers suggestions to facilitate the hands coming to midline. Another example comes later in the child's life when exploration of a classroom leads to an orientation of it. Chapter 3 discusses "exploring time" as a key developmental practice. Each subsequent chapter discusses the process in which the child develops familiarization before orientation, whether it is with the child's own body and the object world (chapter 2), orienting to places (chapter 3) or using the cane for independent movement and travel (chapter 4).

Echolocation

An excellent example of "differences aren't deficits" is the use of echolocation in the movement of blind children. Blind babies use echolocation when crawling: slapping a kitchen floor produces sounds in the environment that can be used for orientation purposes. Use of reflected sound is a skill and a strategy that is the most natural thing to blind children but is not employed by sighted children. Although all humans have the ability to develop echolocation, sighted children are less likely to do so because their visual sense provides them with distance information.

Nurturing this development in blind children begins with educating parents about the nature and use of echolocation. Therefore, in early intervention practices with blind babies, parents and professional service providers should be utilized to facilitate the baby's potential for echolocation. In chapter 2, echolocation is discussed more thoroughly with suggestions on how to facilitate its use in blind children.

Alternative Skills of Blindness

Alternative skills of blindness are the nonvisual skills. They are also the skills used by the blind to teach blindness skills. If blind children are given the equal opportunity, practice, and instruction in the alternative skills of blindness at the developmentally appropriate time, they will be equipped as any child to reach their full potential. Blind children need to learn Braille, just as sighted children need to learn print, at an age/stage appropriate time. Blind children need to learn to use the cane to move and travel about independently, like sighted children learn to move and travel in the world using vision. These basic movement and travel skills, and the other nonvisual skills, enable blind children to pursue independent, full and rich lives.

The Promotion Model explores the nonvisual skills from the bottom-up. For example, in chapter 2 developmental progressions in the child are discussed with alternative, nonvisual skills for the blind child. At the point when the sighted child would use vision, the blind child would use a nonvisual skill. We know about many of the nonvisual skills that blind adults use, but less is known about how to adapt the alternative, nonvisual skills for the blind baby and young blind child. The Promotion Model addresses, in a nonconventional way, these alternative skills to facilitate development in the blind child. As concerned adults for the welfare of blind children, we need to partner our resources to further expand and develop a comprehensive body of information on alternative skills for blind children.

In the education of blind children, the alternative skills of blindness are part of the instructional guide of the individualized educational plan. They are part of the blind child's curriculum. Blind children, like sighted children, need instruction and practice to learn their respective skills. Alternative skills of blindness are described throughout the book. Chapter 5 illustrates such skills with photos.

Using Nonvisual Skills for the Partially Sighted Child

In the development of all babies, touch is used to orient to the body before vision is efficient to use. We can facilitate this natural process for blind babies, whether totally blind or partially sighted, who will not have vision or visual efficiency to observe their independent movement and travel.

Therefore, succeeding with partial sight occurs when the blind child is taught alternative, nonvisual skills of blindness. We can think of it this way for partially sighted children; they have vision for what can be seen and nonvisual skills for what cannot be observed visually.

Practices for learning nonvisual skills, such as using sleep shades (blindfolds), discussed later in this chapter and chapter 3, will facilitate age/stage appropriate skill development. Learning to use the cane for independent movement and travel will place the partially sighted child at an advantage over the partially sighted child who does not learn to use the cane. When we expect partially sighted, legally blind children to compete with their sighted peers without teaching them the nonvisual skills as well, we can make them vulnerable to not learning age/stage appropriate skills. Having at best only 10% of typical vision, legally blind children need to learn the nonvisual skills of blindness so that they can compete and develop on terms of equality with their typically sighted peers. Each subsequent chapter gives examples of nonvisual skills partially sighted children will need to learn.

Early Start With the Cane Travel

The cane will be the most valuable tool for blind children to move, explore, and travel. It is an extension of their sense of touch that puts them in contact with the world around them. It gives children preview and a chance to plan ahead for how the body will be moved. It will be the primary travel tool children will use throughout life. Blind children are best to begin this practice early in life, before they can be influenced by negative attitudes about blindness.

Parents of sighted children would not delay buying a prescription pair of glasses for their child to see. Parents of blind children, however, will think more than twice about their child beginning to use a cane. I believe this is so because they are usually not offered positive, clear, reliable, and useful information about the cane. Using a cane *is* the blind child's *way of seeing*. Delaying the start of the cane is tied to the conventional approach that promotes precane devices as a precursor to the cane. More discussion of the use of the cane early in the blind child's development is presented in chapter 4.

Longer Cane Approach to Travel

From the perspective of the Promotion Model there are three approaches to travel for the blind. There is the *no cane approach,* where the child moves without a cane by holding on to someone else's arm. There is the *shorter cane approach, which is* promoted by conventionally trained O&M professionals who have not embraced the use of alternative cane lengths but rather still apply the same protocols formulated by the Veteran's Administration over half a century ago. And there is the *longer cane approach, which is* promoted by the organized blind and is highly valuable for the independent movement and travel of blind children. The bottom line is that the longer cane approach to travel places the blind child at an advantage over using a shorter cane, and at an even greater advantage over using the no cane approach. Chapter 4 goes into depth about the reasons why the longer cane approach places the child at an advantage.

PRACTICES AND TECHNIQUES

Developmental Adjustment for the Prematurity Event

A baby born severely premature is one of the causes of blindness. We need to have a standardized way of acknowledging and factoring in the impact of the prematurity event on the development of these babies born usually under 26 weeks gestation. The developmental delay caused by the prematurity event needs to be adjusted by professional service providers to more accurately provide appropriate early intervention practices. For example, the baby may be 18 months of age but functioning at 13 months developmentally. Our early intervention needs to be targeted at the developmental level of the child and not the chronological age.

By standardizing the adjustment for prematurity, we will have a more uniform perception of the development of the blind baby. Presently, early intervention program professional service providers adjust for prematurity until 18 to 24 months. These severely premature babies, however, need to have their development adjusted for a longer period of time. For example, being born at 23 to 24 weeks gestation, which is the time frame that many of the blind babies are born, results in 4- to 5-month hospital stays in the neonatal intensive care unit. The early birth, hospital experience and development in the first year of life is significantly affected and, as professional service providers, we need to understand this impact in the first years of life.

When we drop the adjustment for prematurity too early, we create a perception that the baby is more developmentally delayed than is actually the case. This causes us to lower our expectations for the baby and this is conveyed to the parents, who are vulnerable to perceptions of low expectations because their baby is blind as well. Prematurely dropping the adjustment for prematurity perpetuates the perception of the blind baby as being more delayed than is truly the case. We do not need to add to societal misconceptions about blindness that result in lowered expectations for the blind child. Information regarding a more realistic adjustment for the premature event can be found in chapters 2 and 3.

Parent as the Child's First Ground

The meaningful and nurturing interaction between parent and child calls for more touch experiences for the blind baby—holding, feeding, cleansing, massaging, and generally loving the baby. Blind babies, totally blind, or partially sighted, will need more touch experiences in the first years of life to develop emotionally, socially, cognitively, and physically. The type of sensory experiences the children have will formulate the types of concepts that they will develop from those sensory experiences.

One practice that promotes the curiosity, sensory, and motor development is when the "parent is the child's first ground." By this I mean that parents, while lying on their backs, place their baby on their chest and stomach areas. This touch interaction between parent and child encourages the pushing up by the baby on the chest. The upper trunk of the baby's body is used to explore their "first ground," the parent. Through such exploration, the baby develops the appropriate components of movement. Similar exploration may not occur when the baby is placed on the floor, which is not as interesting a space as the parent's chest. Using the parent as the child's first ground is further developed in chapter 2.

Furnish the Midline Space

All babies go through developmental progressions. One progression is the discovery of the hands at the midline space (the chest area) and gradual use of the hands to touch, explore and manipulate the other body parts. This is important for setting the stage to reach off body to objects in the world.

The development of blind babies can be facilitated by alternative skills to enrich the midline area for self-exploration by the baby. This practice of "furnishing the midline space" was offered by Dr. McCune as a way to address such exploration for all babies. Blind babies need to use tactile information whereas sighted babies use visual. For example, we can structure the infant seat with towels on the side so the blind baby's arms are closer in to the body and the baby's hands are more likely to touch each other. Addressing the baby's exploration of the body by furnishing the midline space with objects and activities will facilitate typical development. More discussion of furnishing the midline space can be found in chapters 2 and 3.

Teaching Cane

One practice that I developed while working with blind babies was the use of the "teaching cane." I experimented with this practice by observing blind O&M instructors teaching students cane travel and thought about how it might be applied with blind babies. What follows is an example of how the teaching cane can be used to introduce the baby to the cane. This approach can also be used with toddlers and preschoolers who are more tentative to holding their own cane when it is initially presented to them.

In this strategy the parent is holding a teaching cane, the length of which goes above the chin, in one hand. In the other arm the parent is holding the blind baby, one who may or may not have yet learned to walk. Because the parent will be moving the cane side to side or tapping it, the baby will naturally be curious about what the parent is holding and begin to explore touching the cane.

As the parent slides and taps the cane, the baby will be amused and repeat and mimic the action, attempting to make the same motions and hear the same sounds of the cane tapping. Gradually, the baby will want to stand on the floor and feel the shaft of the cane further down from where the parent is holding it. As the parent slides and taps the cane, the baby will attempt to do the same. When the parent takes walking steps, the baby will walk, holding on to the cane. Blind parents quite naturally would have their own cane for travel and it can be a teaching cane too.

I use the teaching cane with older blind children as well and encourage parents to use a teaching cane too. For example, the adult can demonstrate, by sliding the cane, how wide the sweep of the cane can be or, by tapping the cane, how wide the coverage (beyond the arms of the traveler) should be. When children are learning to locate a curb with their cane, they may be tentative to approach it. The teaching cane can tap the curb to give children auditory preview of the location of the curb. This is better than the adult saying, "I am standing at the curb," because the sound of the cane is a more natural clue, since children can and will be making the same sound with their cane.

The teaching cane is very useful for the developmentally delayed child who needs more repetition, practice, encouragement, and consistency when learning to use the cane, both at home and school. Whatever the age of the cane traveler, the teaching cane facilitates the learning of independent movement and travel skills. Such a practice of the adult using a teaching cane creates an attunement between the learner and the instructor, be it a professional service provider, a parent of a blind child, a teacher or some other concerned party. Of course, blind O&M instructors will naturally use their own cane for travel as a teaching cane too. More discussion of the teaching cane occurs in chapter 4 and a photo of this strategy can be seen in chapter 5.

Role Release

When O&M professionals share their knowledge with parents, the blind child is more likely to receive much more practice in the skills needed for independent movement and travel. Such a "role release" of the O&M professional's role to parents will facilitate the process of O&M and is part of the respectful partnership between them. This will result in the parent encouraging and being part of practicing with the cane to develop skill proficiency.

In the Promotion Model, O&M professionals do not isolate their work with blind children from parents or school staff—both can be important facilitators in the process of O&M. Instructional assistants and teacher's aides can be educated and trained to practice cane skills with the children as part of their individualized education plan. It is a practice that is applied bottom-up for all developmental levels and skill areas for the blind child to be age/stage appropriate. O&M professionals can share the knowledge and power of their information by releasing their role to others. Role release is discussed more in chapter 4.

Unobtrusive Availability

Dr. McCune's expertise encouraged me to understand the concept of "unobtrusive availability." We want the child to learn the skill but in so doing not be obtrusive in the process. Blind children are intruded on when their bodies are manipulated and manually overdirected. Often tasks are done for them that they can do for themselves and they are not given the opportunity to complete tasks for themselves. Why? Because someone responsible for their care decides to interrupt the children while they are "figuring it out" and show them a different or faster way. They are usually shown in the "hand over hand" conventional approach of teaching blind children.

Each adult comes with a pair of hands. Multiply the number of adults "helping" the child day to day at home and in school by the number of hands and that produces a large total number of hands that are on the child. Instead, we need to be available as a resource but not unnecessarily intrude on the child's space. In the education of the blind, the "hands on the blind child" approach (without the child's permission or understanding) is an excellent example of *obtrusive availability by the adult*. While asking children to place their hands on ours as we demonstrate a task is certainly less invasive, this is no substitute for the child learning to do the task for themselves. To do the task independently, blind children must initiate, monitor, guide and experiment with their *own* movement.

In conventional O&M the sighted/human guide is often the most abused mobility skill, as it is one of the most subtle forms of manipulating the blind child's space. *Sometimes the hardest thing to do is "not to do" for the blind child; adults should provide children with opportunities to learn to do the skill for themselves.* Chapter 3 highlights facilitating independent movement and travel and discusses practices that are obtrusive to promoting such independence, while all chapters address being unobtrusively available to blind children.

Exploring Time

Discovery about the world is likely to occur when children are free to explore, driven by their own curiosity, their own need to know, and drive to move. Blind children explore with purposeful thought and movement, as all children do, when they are given the freedom and time to do so. Making choices, trial and error, experimenting with interactions and objects, and developing good judgment are all part of exploring the world.

Like all children, blind children need exploring time from the bottom-up. Children cannot master their environment if they have not become adequately familiar with it. Since familiarization comes before orientation, blind children must be given the opportunity to explore and learn about their world at every developmental stage. In this way blind children can become familiar with their bodies and other people, places, and things. Orientation will become the more natural product of exploration and discovery rather than a lesson on "how to orient" to a particular space, such as a classroom.

I often recommend that exploring time be built into the child's individualized education plan. In this way it will be part of the child's learning and not a hit or miss consideration. Chapter 2 discusses the progressions in development and gives examples of nonvisual, alternative approaches to facilitate exploring, from the baby's own body to the world beyond arm's reach. Chapter 3 continues the discussion of how to facilitate exploration in early intervention and preschool. Chapter 4 discusses how cane travel for blind children can facilitate exploring the environment.

Learning Daily Living Skills

Cane travel is only one of the daily living skills that blind children need to learn. In fact, learning age/stage appropriate daily living skills is a requirement for all children to become independent. Skills for eating, going to the bathroom, bathing, cleaning the kitchen table, and taking out the garbage should be part of the child's everyday life.

When blind children are taught and encouraged to take an appropriate responsibility for their own care and for daily chores, they are more likely to become proficient in their cane travel skills as well.

Learning daily living skills should be part of the home and school experience. Professional service providers who are knowledgeable in the alternative techniques of blindness can teach blind children such skills. If such instruction is not available for the home environment, parents can observe instruction in the school setting. In this way, expectations will be consistent at home and school. Learning daily living skills promotes responsibility and is part of the process toward independence. Chapter 4 discusses cane travel skills and daily living skills at home and school.

Use of Sleep Shades

A very important example of an alternative practice is the use of sleep shades (blindfolds). Employing sleep shades is a sure way to develop confidence in learning blindness skills. The idea behind the use of sleep shades is this: students will learn the skills thoroughly and efficiently without vision by believing in, relying upon and developing their senses of touch and sound. Sleep shades are used to instruct the skills of blindness.

The use of sleep shades by O&M professionals is not universally agreed on. There are O&M professionals using the conventional approach who do not favor using sleep shades at all, and some who believe in partial occlusion to learn movement and travel skills. On the contrary, those who use sleep shades for full occlusion of vision do so because they believe students will develop a confidence in their use of touch and sound best without employing their partial sight or residual vision. They further believe that blind children will integrate the new nonvisual skills in their knowledge base more efficiently than if they do not use sleep shades. Said differently, not using sleep shades may undermine students' confidence because they will never know whether they learned the skill with or without their vision.

By removing the vision, doubt is removed and confidence is built. After learning a skill in an alternative, nonvisual approach, blind children will be able to exercise better judgment when deciding to use a nonvisual skill or their vision. *Simply stated, sleep shades are not about developing visual skills; instead, they are about developing nonvisual skills. Just as sleep shades are not used to develop visual skills, vision should not be used to develop blindness skills.*

It should also be noted that sleep shade training is used to teach graduate students preparing to be O&M professionals. Hours of coursework are utilized learning to develop independent movement and travel skills without the use of vision by using sleep shades. Why would a strategy of using sleep shades for sighted individuals to learn to be independent in cane travel and other daily living skills not be respected and used for their blind students to learn the same skills? Further discussion of sleep shades can be found in chapter 3.

Promote the Characteristics of the Cane That Place the Child at an Advantage

The independent movement and travel of the blind can be promoted, or not, by the type of travel tool used. The cane is the most used travel tool by the blind. The characteristics of the cane chosen to be used by blind adults or given to blind children can make the difference in placing the traveler at an advantage. Blind children are more likely to have a cane chosen for them, and therefore, they may be placed at a disadvantage by being given an inappropriate travel tool. For example, a cane that is too heavy would compromise the hand functioning of the young child. This would delay skill proficiency and perhaps delay the starting of cane instruction because the professional service provider may assess that the child does not have the strength to use the heavier cane. Lighter canes are easier to use by children because their hands can manipulate the cane with greater ease and proficiency.

That is to say, the structure of the cane relates directly to the function of the cane. We can promote functioning with the cane by promoting characteristics of the cane that are user-friendly and facilitate independent movement and travel in the child. Chapter four discusses the variety of characteristics that facilitate independent movement and travel. This places the child at an advantage over using canes whose characteristics are more obtrusive to learning of travel skills.

Use of the Cane as Readiness for Travel

Use of the cane is part of the readiness for travel. Whatever the age, first time cane users must get connected to the cane and the object world before they will have effective and efficient movement and travel. In adults, this process of getting connected is usually quicker because they have conceptual maturity to engage instruction and employ skills more efficiently. Children spend more time from the bottom-up getting connected to the cane and the object world.

In conventional O&M the cane is often delayed until certain "readiness" is exhibited by the child. Such readiness corresponds to a precane curriculum. For example, the child must know positional concepts, such as up and down, or spatial concepts, such as near and far. On the other hand, if we conceptualize the use of the cane as facilitating readiness, then we realize the child will come to know up and down and near and far by *using the cane*. With this perspective we view the cane as a tool that facilitates readiness and is part of the readiness curriculum. The cane does not come after readiness; rather, it is part of readiness.

When we view the cane in this positive light, we are more likely to put the cane in the hand of the child at an earlier age and promote independent movement and travel. The child is more likely to learn age/stage appropriate movement and travel. Chapter four explores the possibilities of using the cane as readiness for travel.

Use of the Cane in the Prewalking Child

The cane can be used with success with the child who has not yet learned to walk. In the typical development of the blind child, the cane can be introduced when the child is beginning to bang objects. The cane would be fun to bang on the floor or ground. It can be used to contact objects beyond arm's reach, and therefore, facilitate curiosity of the environment. The teaching cane is one way to introduce the cane in a prewalking child to promote interest in such a tool.

Such a teaching practice is useful for the developmentally delayed child as well, who may get stuck, for example, in a pattern of walking by holding on to someone's hand or by using an alternative mobility device for a long time, such as a walker. The walker may have been needed earlier when the components of movement were being developed to walk, but transitioning from the walker to walking without it can be problematic for the developmentally delayed blind child. It has been my experience that the cane has facilitated initial walking in these children who seem to be ready to walk independently but who do not. Therefore, the protocol for using the cane is not always after the child learns to walk. Think about using the cane to facilitate development whether or not the child has achieved the motor milestone of walking. Chapter 4 explores the use of the cane in the nonwalking child.

Use of the Cane to Facilitate Sensory Integration

Because the cane is held in the hand and touches the ground in coordination with the feet, it can facilitate the integration of the use of the upper and lower body simultaneously in movement. Also, using the cane in one hand, at times switching it to the other hand or using one hand to explore while holding the cane in the other, promotes sensory integration of the left and right sides of the body.

Physical and occupational therapists can employ the use of the cane during their therapies with blind children. Such tool usage will facilitate sensory integration, which is one of the goals of therapy. The most significant way to facilitate sensory integration is the daily use of the cane by the child. As part of the child's own active movement and use of sensory information, sensory integration will be promoted.

Functional Skills Assessment

The common label for teachers of the blind and visually impaired is TVI (teachers of the visually impaired). They typically use an assessment tool called a "Functional Vision Evaluation or Assessment." Nationwide this assessment is often used on a totally blind child as well. Ironically, the name does not fit who is being assessed. An exception can be found in Louisiana Tech University's preparatory program for O&M. Their description of teachers of the blind and visually impaired is TBS (teachers of blind students). This program emphasizes the skills of *blindness* regardless of whether the child has any vision or not.

This does not mean that low vision aids and low vision technology are not considered for partially sighted children. But what it does mean is this: the evaluation used is a "Functional Skill Assessment" and it covers *all* areas of development. Vision is only one of the sensory systems available. The assessment tool being used should reflect all available sensory skill areas of the child. One way to reflect this fact is to correctly label the assessment tool.

In the Promotion Model, the name for the assessment is Functional Skills Assessment, as it opens the door of possibilities for what the blind child needs to learn in all areas of development for independent movement and travel. Chapters 2, 3 and 4 present areas of development and skills of blindness to be addressed in the child for any functional skills assessment.

The Criteria Used for the Assessment Should be Predictive of the Outcome

The plan for and goal of assessments in O&M should be for skill proficiency in independent movement and travel. Unfortunately, there are O&M assessment tools that do not serve the best interests of the child. In conventional O&M there have been a number of assessments developed that will keep blind children busy with an O&M professional all through their early intervention and preschool years and not one criteria for assessment will be about the cane. The precane skills and precane devices blind children are taught in the curricula that follow these assessments have very little to do with predicting independent movement and travel.

The criteria used for the assessment should always be *predictive* of the outcome and this should be independence in movement and travel. For example, there have been pages and pages written about the sighted/human guide technique with specific instructions for assessment, instruction and behavioral outcomes. Much valuable learning time can be "made" of teaching the guided techniques, but what does learning these skills have to do with the child learning about *independent movement and travel?* Instead, blind children need to learn to self-initiate, monitor, sustain, and terminate their own movement. They do this by moving and traveling solo in the world.

Assessments for the O&M of young blind children must include use of the cane. Without it, such an assessment is incomplete and not predictive of its goal. The functional skills for independent movement and travel in blind children are discussed in each chapter. These skills are the criteria that will produce the outcome we want for blind children, which is the independence to be full participants in society.

THE BUILDING BLOCKS OF THE PROMOTION MODEL WORK TOGETHER

The building blocks of the Promotion Model have been offered as a package—a holistic design of philosophy, developmental perspectives, strategies for teaching, and practices to implement those strategies to facilitate the independent movement and travel in blind children. When we remove a building block, it will alter the intent and interconnectedness of the package being presented.

For example, if parents are not respected as the child's first O&M teacher, this affects so many other building blocks. For instance:

- This will result in limited experiences in parents having informed choice.
- The child is less likely to have an early start to cane travel that can be promoted at home.
- The teaching cane may not be known or promoted by the parent, and therefore, not be introduced.
- Role release of information so parents can more effectively practice cane skills with their child will be hindered.
- The positive influence parents can have on their children taking an appropriate age/stage responsibility for their own travel will be reduced.
- The importance of learning daily living skills to facilitate general independence and the use of the cane may not be realized.

If we include the parent as the child's first teacher all the aforementioned building blocks are more likely to be positively affected.

Using all the building blocks together make for the best recipe for success in the independent movement and travel of blind children. In using any tested and reliable recipe, I do acknowledge human variation in style of presentation. For example, when making an apple pie we may add some cinnamon and brown sugar, and be creative with the crust design, but we *will* remember that without apples, it is not an apple pie. Therefore, it is understood that the child, the parent, the professional service provider, school personnel, and other interested parties will each bring a personal style and creativity to the building blocks being presented.

THE ROLE OF THE ORIENTATION
AND MOBILITY PROFESSIONAL

This chapter started with an explanation of O&M and will end with a description of the O&M professional's role when utilizing the Promotion Model.

The Promotion Model outlined in this chapter is meant to provide O&M professional service providers with the principles, developmental perspectives, strategies, practices, and techniques that will facilitate independent movement and travel in blind children. The Promotion Model is designed to be a positive approach for the field of O&M. As someone who has provided O&M services for many years, I believe the role of O&M professionals can and do bring a positive, hopeful message and reliable developmental guidance to the parents of blind children. I also believe that O&M professionals can bring, although unintentionally, a fear based, if not tentative, introduction to the idea of independent movement and travel to the parents of blind children. O&M professionals with positive information about blindness and the skills of blindness are more likely to deliver a positive, confident and hopeful message to parents.

The O&M specialist working with blind children will function as an "orientation and mobility architect," analyzing the needs of children to design a plan that will produce independence in movement and travel. Working with parents and the school, including early intervention and preschool, the O&M professional will implement strategies that will facilitate preparing the child for present and future independent movement and travel. The O&M specialist's role may fluctuate between consultant, demonstrator, and ongoing instructor. Of particular importance will be providing parents with clear, accurate information about blindness. The *attunement* between parent and child will be the foundation for the child getting to know and move in the world. The O&M specialist will evaluate what is available to the child and give developmental guidance for this attunement.

In partnership with parents, the O&M specialist will explore strategies, activities, and tools to facilitate purposeful thought and movement. By being more aware of our "menu," we will "feed" blind children experiences that will make sense to them. In this way, the more natural course and intent of maturation may unfold over time. For example, cane travel will not be viewed as an isolated set of skills, but as part of a process, a progression of learning manipulative skills. The spoon, then, becomes a natural precursor to the cane. Tools used to manage space and get tasks done (such as spoons, scoops, shovels, and brooms) will be utilized in the bottom-up approach. *The alternative skills of blindness will be "thought out" and applied from infancy to adulthood.*

The O&M specialist will be cautious not to prematurely insist on proper adult-centered techniques, as this may interrupt the young child's need to explore, figure it out, and develop useful self-taught solutions. As O&M specialists, we must invite blind children to explore and discover the world and come to understand that it is a friendly and interesting place. We must encourage children to make the world their home, to move safely, confidently, and effectively, and to demonstrate the kind of strength, wisdom, and poise that is within them.

CHAPTER 2

DEVELOPMENTAL PROGRESSIONS IN THE CHILD

A child playing in a tunnel-barrel-drum
and enjoying echoes and movement.

Independent Movement and Travel in Blind Children: A Promotion Model, pp. 53–91
Copyright © 2007 by Information Age Publishing

*If you can just observe what you are and move with it, then you will
find that it is possible to go infinitely far.*
                          —J. Krishnamurti

All children move through stages of development and
acquire new skills at each stage. The skills build upon one
another and this progressive development results in
increasing independence of the child. The progressions
outlined below represent a range of behaviors in the early
skilled action of *all* children, from infancy to the school
age child. Progressions in development of the child
express this drive for a higher level of organization of
experiences.

In the typical child these developmental progressions
are formed during the first 3 years of life. One definition
of a baby is a child who is under 3 years of age. This is the
operating definition I am using in the Promotion Model.
Research on the acquisition of learning new skills illustrates that *the baby is a creator and an organizer.* For example,
when we observe more complex movement of the blind
baby, we realize how the blind baby develops and utilizes
echolocation from precrawling, crawling, walking, and
using the cane. We can appreciate the sequence of organization, reorganization and more efficient use of echolocation.

Awareness of the existence of these progressions in
development of *all* children and their implications for the
independent movement and travel for the blind child will
encourage a more meaningful menu of experiences that
we can offer to the blind baby in our early intervention. In
the description below of these progressions, "typical"
developmental guidelines are given with some examples
of alternative skills useful during the developmental stage
being discussed. We want to promote movement that leads
to exploration, discovery, experimentation, play, and

eventually mastery over the environment. We want to ensure that blind babies keep appropriately busy in what interests *them* and nurtures their development. Nature has intended developmental progressions and it is our role to facilitate nature's intent for the child.

The amount of information to be organized in early childhood development can be a cumbersome task for parents and professional service providers to highlight and target the needs for the blind child's independent movement and travel. My organization of *what we know* about child development into these progressions is offered as a way to simplify and more clearly understand child development and how it relates to independent movement and travel. It is my hope that you will find this conceptualization useful.

Role of Professional Service Provider

The role of the professional service provider is to supply parents with information about the developmental progressions in the child. The orientation and mobility (O&M) specialist will emphasize the importance of active movement and independent travel and provide developmental guidance to parents regarding the age/stage appropriate alternative skills of blindness. Imparting such information requires the O&M specialist to be part of the early intervention "team" visiting the home of the parent and/or at a center-based program. Early intervention practices regarding facilitating active movement and independent exploration and travel are discussed in chapter 3.

O&M specialists and other early intervention service providers will model appropriate alternative skills for parents. The professional service provider shows parents the what and how of their intervention practices so that the parents can follow through day to day with facilitating the development of their child. This *role release* of information creates a meaningful partnership between parents and professionals that benefits the child's development.

Role of the Parent

Research on early childhood development indicates that early intervention works best when parents are involved with the guiding and teaching of their child. The involvement of the parent is so central to the outcome of what and how the child will learn. The Promotion Model describes the parent and child as "one unit." When parents believe they can affect the outcome of what and how their child will learn, they are more likely to be involved in the early intervention *teaching* of their child.

In the Promotion Model the parent *is the child's first teacher.* Professional service providers facilitate the empowerment of parents to interact and be involved in their child's learning alternative skills of blindness. The age/stage developmental progressions of the child are more likely to occur when parents are fueling, nurturing, and guiding their child's daily activities.

Parents will be involved with all of the developmental progressions that are described in this chapter. Examples are given of how to facilitate development and nurture the child's *need to know and drive to move* for each developmental progression. The love that parents have for their child can be given a *structure of involvement* that can produce positive outcomes for independent movement and travel. Parents play a vital role in their child's development.

The Development of Our Spatial Sense

In order to expand the understanding of our role in facilitating movement, I will give a brief explanation of our "spatial sense," which gives us knowledge about where we are in space and what we are doing with our bodies in that space. Through such an understanding of the main components in spatial perception, we can more clearly understand what activities will nurture developmental progressions in blind children.

Understanding our position or where we are in space is needed so that we can understand and plan our movements. Planning our movements may be as simple as sitting down or standing up, moving fast or slow, or may be more complex, such as knowing how to circumvent an obstacle—go around, under, or over it. In orientation and mobility (O&M), travelers need more advanced spatial information to step down from a curb, cross a street, and then know their position in space to plan their next part of their journey.

As human beings, there are three main ways of knowing where we are in the spatial world. The ways of knowing spatial orientation are based primarily on three sensory systems, the tactile (touch), auditory (hearing and balance mechanisms in the inner ear), and visual (sight). The terms used by professionals to describe these systems have technical names. My purpose is not to get distracted by jargon but rather, keep it simple to understand the essence of these three systems. Let me give a brief explanation for these systems. The Resources chapter gives suggestions for finding more technical information about these spatial systems.

The tactile system has to do with the contracting and stretching of muscles, compressing the joints between the bones, and attaining different body positions (bending, straightening, pulling). There are receptors on and under the skin and in the body that convey information about touch and movement to the brain. This information sent to the brain is about "feeling" our movement or the position of our body. For example, if I close my eyes and someone moves my right arm at a 90-degree angle from the trunk of my body (out to my side) and then I am asked to repeat the same action and position with my left arm, I can do so. I was able to sense the movement (muscles, joints, position) of my right arm; the information is sent to the brain and the directions are sent out from the brain to do the same action to my left arm. You can understand the lack of coordination that may result if my left arm can not tell what the right arm is doing. If this were the case, the tactile system would not be working properly.

The auditory system gives us hearing. It also provides us with the mechanisms in the inner ear that contribute to our understanding of our body's position in space. Changes in position and movement are registered in this elaborate inner ear system and information forwarded to the brain. The brain processes this information and sends messages to the body. For example, if we "feel" a sense of falling backward, then we react by moving forward or in some other way to correct the imbalance.

We understand the impact of hearing loss for the deaf child. Less understood, however, is the impact for the normal hearing blind child who may have some type of inner ear dysfunction that does not affect hearing but rather balance or some other type of dysfunction of "feeling" the body's position in space. An understanding of the inner ear's role in the spatial orientation of the deaf child would direct professional service providers for the proper therapy and interventions. The hearing blind child may be vulnerable, however, to misconceptions about the innate balance of blind children and the inner ear dysfunction may go undiagnosed in favor of the professional thinking it's a "blindness" issue. This thinking would result in the blind child not getting the proper therapy to address the real problem, which is in the inner ear.

The visual system has to do with sight, the ability to see objects and scan/track them with our eye(s). People who are legally blind have a visual acuity of 20/200 or less in the better eye after correction or a visual field of 20 degrees or less. By definition their vision is only 10% of typical vision (20/20). This reduced amount of vision will have an effect on how the visual system will function in regards to providing accurate information about where they are in space and doing visual tasks.

What are the implications for movement if one of these systems is not working at all or only partially? We know totally blind children function without the visual system and that partially sighted children function with a reduced effectiveness of this system (see also "Succeeding with Partial Sight" in chapter 3). The deaf-blind child may or may not have complete functioning of the inner ear but certainly will not be able to see and hear very well or at all. Fortunately, the blind child (totally or partially sighted) and the deaf-blind child (totally or partially deaf/sighted) will most likely have *full access* to the tactile system. *This is good news because the sense of touch is part of the tactile system, which is the largest sensory system in humans.* It is vital that we understand the value and significance of touch for the blind child, and most certainly the deaf-blind child, if we are to create a developmental approach that will facilitate the progressions outlined in this chapter.

In the Promotion Model the tactile/touch system is valued as the most important sensory system. Because of this system the *body has an "eye on itself" from the inside that observes and regulates movement.* What *is* essential for babies is what the brain observes, not what the eye can see. How babies and older children are interpreting and using touch will greatly influence their movement to develop their early skills. Our tactile/touch system is the oldest system to develop in evolutionary terms. In other words, it was the first to develop. Touch is the sense that develops first and foremost in utero and, when the baby is born, is the most developed sense available to the baby. Our skin is our largest organ. A most significant part of the brain is devoted to the hand. The brain is an equal opportunity employer that needs to get information verified, and therefore, will rely upon this sense of touch *more* than partial sight (or partial hearing in the deaf child).

We know from research, for example, that the Braille finger has a corresponding growth pattern in the brain for that finger. The deaf child will develop areas of the visual cortex usually assigned to the auditory part of the brain. *Early on in the development of the child, the brain is very flexible. The brain is not wasteful. It is efficient and uses what the child has and has most of—the sense of touch.*

Therefore, in our understanding of the progressions in development, it is vital to understand the role that tactile/touch system will play in the blind child's development. This will better equip us to promote independent movement and travel in blind children. This understanding of the importance of touch for blind children will fuel our interest and motivation to create alternative techniques for blind children, from the bottom-up, that facilitate age/stage appropriate development.

Passive Movement to Active Movement

Where does movement begin? One answer is that movement starts in the womb of the mother. When the mother moves there is movement of the baby. Everywhere the mother goes there is movement, movement, movement! Gradually the baby initiates its own movement. We can understand the interruption of this intended movement pattern in premature birth. This vulnerability for the blind child who is born premature will be covered later in this chapter and in chapter 3.

When the baby is born there is no longer continual movement with the mother. Here we can understand the invention of baby carriers and the idea of "wearing your baby."

In the first year of life we can understand the process of "we do it for you, then with you and then you do it alone." Adults initially give more touch affections and touch prompts to babies and gradually reduce their touch interactions. We gradually give more verbal information and prompts as the baby becomes more active in movement.

As Dr. Lilli Nielsen has suggested, one way of describing passive movement is when we initiate the movement, when the thought for movement comes from the adult's brain. Active movement is when the child initiates the movement and the thought for movement comes from the child's brain. Not only in the early years, but also throughout life as well, when we are learning something new we progress from a greater reliance upon passive movement to more active movement.

Think back to when we learned to drive, take a bus, skate, ski, or learn any new skill. We initially needed more guidance and information and gradually developed a complete self-monitoring, mastery of the skill. In order to promote independent movement and travel in blind children it is important for adults to know when and how to facilitate active movement in the child.

Movement Develops From Head to Foot and From the Trunk of the Body to the Hands

Development in utero, and out of the womb in the first year of life moves from head to foot. This is significant for the blind child, as the hands and feet will be the last to develop motor skill proficiency in the first year of life. The development of typical life skills by the blind child will require foot travel and the integrity of hand use, and yet the blind child is quite vulnerable to delays in development that may affect use of these perceptual organs.

For example, sometimes a baby can get "stuck" in a position and not advance easily to the next motor progression. A baby on the stomach, who could be pushing up from the floor, may have the arms in back in a more premature position called the "swimmer's position." If this baby is ready for a more advanced position but is stuck in such a position, the arms may need to be facilitated to be in front, touching some interesting object that would encourage a higher level use of the hands and arms.

We must ensure that our alternative skills meet the needs of the blind child in developing the movement components that set the stage for hand and finger manipulation and control of balance and exploring with the feet. In chapter 5 many examples of alternative skills are given to facilitate such movement.

Movement Proceeds From Reflexive to Accidental to Intentional

In very early movement in all babies there are *reflexes* (involuntary movement). These movements introduce the baby to more voluntary and active movement. For instance, in the first few months of life one such reflex is the asymmetrical tonic neck reflex. This has been referred to as the "fencing position." When the baby is on the back and the head is turned to the right, the right arm will be extended out to that side and the left arm is bent at the elbow with the hand near the head. The sighted baby *may* be visually regarding the right hand or the fingers moving and getting visual preview of what will become a very important part of the child's body, the hand.

What is interesting to note in this position, although the baby may be facing (looking) in the direction of its right arm/hand, is that the left hand moves. Could this be a sign of the eventual involvement, the "wired in" inter-connectedness of the right and left hands? Of course, I am conjecturing here about the possible wired in intent of the baby. But what is not conjecturing is this: *when blind babies (and even partially sighted babies whose vision is not developed during the time of this reflex) are in the fencing position and the arm is extended, they are not getting the possibility of visual pre-view.*

So, would it be reasonable to stimulate the hand(s) with touch affections and play with blind babies in this position so that they get a "touch" preview of what is at the end of their arm? Might this be an equivalent experience from the brain's point of view for information? I would suggest this *is* a technique to promote an alternative skill, from the bottom-up perspective.

Reflexes gradually give way to more observations and beginnings of purposeful use of the body by the baby. Babies experience *"accidental"* observations, as in the sighted babies seeing the hand pass their field of view. Gradually these accidental observations lead to experimentation, more purposeful and then intentional use of vision to ensure the hands find each other when in the field of view.

An alternative skill for the blind baby to observe the hands accidentally occurs when we create environments where the hands are more likely to be observed. We can put towels, for example, at the sides of the baby's body when in an infant seat to prop up the elbows and bring the hands closer to one another so that the hands are more likely to touch one another. Or perhaps when the mother is breast feeding a little milk can be put on the palm of the hands of the baby; in turn, the baby by smelling the milk will bring its hands together at the face.

From behaviors generated by reflexes, to an increase in accidental observations and beginnings of purposeful behavior of the baby, develops more and more *intentional* actions. Babies begin to roll, push up on their stomachs, bring their hands the middle of their body, and discover their feet. Like all babies, blind babies will develop in this same progression if we adults promote touch and sound affections and active movement to facilitate nature's intent.

Purposeful thought and movement come together in intentional actions of the baby. The baby is *motivated* by the interactions with the parents. Motivation plays a key role in the development in intentional actions. This is where the perception and actions of the parent, as the child's first teacher, fuels and motivates the baby to explore and experiment with increasingly more complex intentional actions.

REACHING AND SEARCHING

In the development of babies there is "on body" contact and exploration before "off body" contact with the world. The precursor to reaching *off* body is the tactile connection *on* body first—one body part touching another part of the body. This applies to all children. Then the baby begins to reach off body, searching for an object, including one that is out of view, hidden or "lost." *With the alternative skills of blindness, blind children can achieve these developmental progressions within the same time frame as their sighted peers.*

On Body Contact

It is interesting to note that in the typical development of sighted babies exploring their bodies is first directed by touch—the babies feel their hands coming together on the chest and exploring their hands. This occurs before vision is used to contact the body part to be explored. At 3 to 4 months the babies discover the hands while on the middle of the chest (known as the midline space). This is very significant because it means that the baby is "wired in," blind or sighted, to connect and explore on the body. This is good news for the blind baby who would want to use touch anyway.

Another way of phrasing this is on body contact, observation and exploring. This is the beginning of reaching; an active movement in the progression of head to foot control, the hand purposefully explores and is beyond a reflex action. Blind babies will reach on their body and explore everything about themselves. They are getting "connected" like all babies get connected to themselves. The possibilities of on body observation are unlimited if we begin to think in alternative ways in the early development of the blind baby. Photos with descriptions of getting connected and the beginnings of contact on body and reaching can be found in chapter 5.

Reaching Off Body

Around 4 to 6 months of age sighted babies reach off body. Sighted babies will learn to reach with vision and blind babies with touch. Both sighted and blind babies use sound to orient to reach. When babies reach toward sound information this is known as "sound localization." When blind babies reach off body to a sound source this has been referred to as "auditory reach." For example, the sighted baby may see and hear a musical toy that the mother is holding and reach for it. The blind baby will hear the music and reach for it. The partially sighted baby may reach visually or not, depending on the validity of the visual information perceived. I have had experiences with totally blind babies using auditory reach between 4 to 6 months, which is the same time period that sighted babies will use their vision and sound to reach.

What is important to know and remember is this: *in the early development of babies, sound has very little meaning without touch.* This fact has even greater impact for blind babies who will need more touch to develop an interest and understanding of an object being explored. *Blind babies need experience with the object making the sound in their hands first to understand that the sound is connected to this object. In this way, when the sound is heard off body they will be more likely to reach for it because it has a prior meaning to them.* Blind and partially sighted babies who do not have vision to see the object will require *more* touch with the object in their hands than sighted babies who are using vision and sound to preview the object.

In infant research of sighted babies there is a concept called "synchrony." This refers to the fact that two senses are used to verify each other. Things to see are things to touch. In the blind baby, things to hear are things to touch. One example of synchrony is the voice-face event. This is when the baby hears the voice of the parent, turns and sees a face. The baby comes to expect to see the face. What of the blind baby who turns to the voice, which blind babies will do, and doesn't see a face? How can we synchronize the event for them? The answer is simple: when the blind baby turns to the parent's voice give them touch and sound affections on the face and the hands and through the ears, respectively.

The above is an example of promoting an alternative skill of two senses validating one another. I remember one blind baby who, when hearing grandma's voice on the telephone and could not touch grandma, then smelled the phone. Perhaps this was an attempt to verify grandma's voice. We want the blind baby to have a second mode of information, just as the sighted baby, to verify the experience. In the Promotion Model, touch is *the* integrating, verifying sense in such early exploration. Chapter 5 illustrates this voice-face event for the blind baby.

Searching for an Object

Babies will search for an object, without a clue or verbal prompt, on the average between 8 to 12 months of age. When a baby searches for an object that is hidden from view—and by this I mean that no sensory clues, verbal or tactile prompts are given by the adult—then the baby is said to have achieved one marker for "object permanence." This is the knowing that an object exists without observing its presence. What is interesting to note is that *with all the advantages to having sight, the typical sighted baby does not develop object permanence any sooner than the typical blind baby.*

From the point of view of the Promotion Model, the beginnings of object permanence and searching for objects in the world, and the exploring the environment that follows, starts with *person permanence: the baby is looking for the parent.* The baby's reaching and calling for mother and father is *the precursor to object permanence, and subsequently the engagement with the object world.* Once again, we can see the value of the parents as the child's first teacher since person permanence precedes object permanence. As human beings, we are interested in human "objects" first and then nonhuman objects second.

FAMILIARIZATION BEFORE ORIENTATION

What we observe in a baby's getting to know and move in the world is a familiarization before orientation, first with the baby's body and then with the environment. We can observe such a progression in becoming oriented in the object world. For example, in becoming oriented, infant research has illustrated the following: a period of *attending* to an object, then a period of *experimenting* with it and finally *triggering* a response to it. The baby may see or touch an object accidentally, then begin swatting at it and finally grabbing it.

Blind children will observe, connect, coordinate, and orient to their world if they have the opportunities to engage in activities that make sense to them. In the progression of familiarization to orientation we observe the child getting connected to the object world in a gradually more purposeful and creative way.

Dr. Lilli Nielsen's Little Room is an excellent example of a *play space to learn to orient within*. Such a play space has been referred to as an "environmental intervention." The Little Room uses materials to accentuate resonance, vibration and tactile feedback, thus affording opportunities created by its structure and function.

In *Early Learning, Step by Step* Dr. Nielsen offers an abundance of information not only about development in normal and severely delayed in blind children, but also in offering materials and environments to facilitate getting connected, getting familiar, and developing mastery over the object world. This book is listed in the Resources Section.

Sensory Before Conceptual

For the young child, out of the experience comes the concept. This is the essence of the bottom-up approach, which is an integral part of the Promotion Model. This is another way of talking about the sensory and motor processes in children to get to know and move in the world, to get *enough* experience gathering, integrating, and thinking about this information. Ultimately, we want blind children to think that they can "go to the world," visit it, and make it their home.

Babies move first within their own body space (reflexes and voluntary). Then they develop an understanding of their body (connecting first by on body exploration and then reaching off body). Developing next is the use of "object space" (their relationship of self to the object world), followed by an understanding of the relationships of objects to other objects. And finally, they develop map space (symbolic representations of self to the world). Blind babies must be provided opportunities to partake in this process. This can happen if opportunity, developmental guidance, and appropriate materials and tools are given to the child.

The first and most important sensory experiences will be the result of the interaction between parent and child. Through the touch and sound affections the parent gives the blind baby, a "sense of other" begins to develop. One of the first ways to know when person permanence is occurring is in tickling. When a baby laughs to being tickled by someone this demonstrates awareness of the "other." When we try tickling ourselves, it's not the same feeling because we know we are doing it. Parents must reach in and become very playful and involved with their blind baby. Too much time lying in a crib is not a good thing. The blind baby needs to listen in more active environments.

It is important to note that in the development of sighted babies, research has shown that parents move further and further away from the play of their baby, usually in the second year of life. The attunement across space can be conveyed visually. This type of facial expression attunement is not available for blind and partially sighted children, so sound must be relied upon across distance. Because at first sound has very little meaning without touch, you will know, as the parent or the O&M specialist, if verbal input across a room is registering with the blind baby. If not, more touch will be needed closer in before moving further away.

Blind children who do not get enough experience to make "sense out of it all" can become conceptually confused, withdrawn, or develop frequently repeated behaviors such as eye poking, constant turning, and rocking. These children are vulnerable to not developing to full capacity in their independent movement and travel. However, when blind babies are given adequate and appropriate sensory experiences, then over time they will develop and understand sensory experiences and begin to think about and develop speech and language and concepts about the world.

Tool Usage: From the Spoon to the Cane

Blind children need to learn daily living skills and the tools that are needed to perform these skills. For children, toys are their tools also. This underscores the importance that play provides, a skilled and organized approach to experiment and interact with the world. The baby will want to play with all the tools, first banging, then tapping and exploring. That's what babies do. Once again, look toward "normal" development to guide you in this area of tool usage. Dr. Nielsen suggests giving blind babies a cane to bang when they are at the developmental stage of banging objects. If the idea is not obvious on how to approach the learning of a skill with the blind child then seek information about the alternative skill that is required. *Remember that there is always an alternative and there is always a solution.*

Sometimes a blind baby will be introduced to a cane at 1 to 3 years of age and may not want anything to do with it. This will be demonstrated by pushing it away, saying "no" or some other such behavior. There can be several reasons for this. For example, upon discussion with the parent it is discovered that the child has not learned to use the spoon or any eating utensil. This child is accustomed to the spoon coming to the mouth by another person; therefore, the spoon is for *someone else* to use. Such experience with using eating tools needs to be learned in an age/stage appropriate way.

Tool usage is a set of skilled actions to get a job done that involve problem-solving skills. Such skills will benefit the child throughout life. Activities and tools that facilitate daily living skills develop purposeful thought and movement, as well as invite the child to be amused, explore, experiment, create and guide behavior to be more active and less passive.

PROGRESSIONS IN MOTOR DEVELOPMENT

Most research on blind children indicates and concludes that blindness in itself is the reason there are delays in acquisition of motor milestones and the transitioning to and from these milestones. From the Promotion Model perspective it is the missing components of movement that cause the delay, not blindness. Much of the research targets pushing up in prone and walking as the greatest delay areas. What none of these studies explain, however, is why there are blind babies and blind children who develop without a problem, who develop "normally."

Some of these blind children that develop within normal, typical developmental guidelines have never experienced early intervention or preschool programs targeted at their blindness, their perceived deficit. How can this be? The answer is simply this: *blindness in itself is not the cause of the problem and does not need to be fixed. What should be addressed are the alternative skills blind children will need to develop as a typical child.*

Below is a brief discussion of the major motor milestones with some thoughts for consideration for blind children. I begin with a discussion of the blind baby born prematurely and then move on to discuss the typical development of sighted and blind babies. General guidelines in months are given only as a reference. What is most important is not the particular month the baby may partake in the activity but that the baby does develop the components of movement that comprise the motor skill. The sequence of development is critical, not the particular month in which it occurs. In the typical development of the blind baby there will be a range of age for acquisition of a skill, as there is in the development of the sighted baby. Chapter 5 will illustrate with photos a number of alternative skills to facilitate the motor development of blind babies.

Premature Development

Full-term babies are folded up when they are born. In typical development, the baby unfolds like a little flower and then gradually the hands are brought to the center (midline) of the body in the chest area. This happens during the first 2 to 3 months of life. Babies who are born premature do not experience full folding and pressure in the womb. In addition they have spent months in the hospital splayed out and toneless. Part of the hospital experience is to fold the baby as it would have been in utero had the baby not been prematurely born. When brought home these babies often need time to unfold, as if they were just born. The result of the premature birth, the hospital experience and the need to develop (unfold) should be taken into consideration.

The standard protocol for premature babies is that they will catch up by 18 months to 2 years of age. From the Promotion Model point of view, this conventional protocol does not truly take into account the type of severe premature birth these blind babies experience. These babies are often born between 23 and 26 weeks gestation. The fact is that these babies are rewriting the medical books. Their severe premature birth, combined with their lengthy institutionalized experience in the hospital, should be properly reflected in the "adjustment" of their chronological age. I prefer to subtract the number of weeks premature and then subtract the weeks in the hospital from the chronological age and this should give the *corrected age*. This could be 7, 8, 9 months or more. This gives us a better corrected birth date to measure the baby's development.

Let me give an example with educational implications. A baby born at 24 weeks is born 4 months (16 weeks) early (40 weeks gestation less 16 weeks premature equals 4 months). This baby was in the hospital for 5 months (20 weeks). The 4 months premature plus 5 months in the hospital is a total of 9 months adjustment from the chronological age. Let's say the baby is 16 months chronologically. By subtracting 9 months, this would mean the *adjusted age* is 7 months.

A developmental assessment by the professional service provider shows that the baby is sitting up independently and overall development is about 6 to 8 months. Is this baby's development delayed, normal, or advanced? The answer greatly depends on perception. Perception of the baby's development depends on the adjustment for prematurity. If the professional adjusts only 4 months, then the baby is delayed. If the adjustment is 9 months, then the baby is within the norm, perhaps slightly ahead in some areas of development. And if the professional has dropped the adjustment, then the baby is perceived to be severely delayed. My position is this: if we are to err on the adjustment, then let the error be in favor of the baby, which would be the 9 months adjustment in this case. It is also important to *never drop the adjusted age during the early intervention and preschool years.*

Often in early intervention programs the adjusted age will be dropped by 18 months to 2 years of age. The *perception* of developmental delay(s) in these severely premature babies will be more negative. You can imagine the kind of research conclusions one would get by examining blind babies born at 23 weeks gestation and not adjusting appropriately for their premature birth. Parents and professional service providers must make clear to early intervention staff and school district personnel the realistic adjustment for severe prematurity. The baby transitions out of early intervention into preschool based on chronological age. The adjustment should go with the baby into childhood. Usually the adjustment is dropped and then the perceived delay will appear even greater. This will have implications for how the school district will perceive the child's abilities and what programs they will recommend.

One program for the care of premature babies is especially helpful for blind babies. It is called Kangaroo Care and comes from South America. The idea is taken from the way mother kangaroos carry their babies in the mother's pouch. The Kangaroo Care proponents recommend "wearing the premature baby," breastfeeding and sleeping in the upright position with the baby. The mother sleeps sitting up lying against a pillow. Under her nightgown, touching her chest, the baby is cradled. The idea is that the baby needs movement of the kind it missed in the mother's womb. Research shows that babies who received Kangaroo Care had better weight gain and overall growth than those premature babies who did not partake in the program. This idea makes a lot of sense and is not unlike a number of cultures in this world where babies are "worn" for many months after they are born.

On the Back Baby

After the first few months of life when they have unfolded, babies seem to enjoy being on their backs, observing the world. (The technical term for this position is "supine.") On their backs, after the first few months of life, the babies bring their hands on their chest and begin to explore the hands. From a month the babies further explore the knees, legs, and feet. Eventually the babies bring their feet to their mouths. This is important because this position "simulates" what will become later in the upright position, sitting. While lying on their backs, things to feel are things to grab.

Rotation of the trunk begins as babies start reaching off body and often they turn onto the stomach. On the back, the blind baby is listening to the sound space world. Often, what may be observed as the blind baby doing "very little" could be active listening to the environment or the hand reaching under a blanket to actively explore.

A baby lying on its back can enjoy the Little Room promoted by Dr. Lilli Nielsen. This play space brings the ceiling down to the baby, and by the suspension of objects the baby can reach and play with them. The Little Room is placed on a Resonance Board, which brings echoes close at hand and foot. The baby enjoys banging the feet and using the hand to explore and bang objects to make sounds. This is a much more stimulating environment than the crib for the blind baby, where the mattress is soft, the ceiling high and the resonance is much less.

On the Stomach Baby

The baby facing the floor while on the stomach, also called the "prone" position, is a very important position because it prepares the baby for a greater variety of movement possibilities when sitting. For example, in the first 6 months of life, the on the stomach baby learns to prop up on its forearms, and gradually learns to bear weight on extended forearms, push up, pivot, and turn. From this position the baby can begin to eventually reach, resting on one forearm while reaching with the other hand. Babies can demonstrate lying on their side and hand to mouth play. During this time the baby is developing good head control, recognizes voices of parents, and sits with support. Some blind babies are very active and keep up with their sighted peers while others are less active. *The opportunity to take part in and enjoy the on the stomach position is likely to occur if it is an interesting place to be.*

This is where "chest-to-chest" play comes in, where the baby is on the parent's chest, pushing up from the parent's chest, exploring the parent and the close *face-to-face space* of the parent. In this way, the parents can be thought of as the *first ground* of the blind baby. Instead of sounds coming only from above the baby, in this position the baby experiences sound coming from below. With the touch and sound sensations in this position (chest-to-chest), on the stomach becomes a much more interesting space to move in and explore. It is also a space in which the blind baby can experience rolling over from belly to back. This alternative skill of chest-to-chest makes the on the stomach experience much more enjoyable for the blind baby. The components of movement experienced in this position will be built upon in the next motor milestone, sitting.

It is very important during this time to furnish the midline space. We must think of ways to make the chest area of the body interesting to the blind baby, where the hands will meet and explore. One grandmother I know attached Velcro to her grandchild's t-shirt and attached little sound making items to the chest area of it so that when the baby moved and heard the sounds, discovering the objects at midline was easy and pleasing. Chapter 5 gives examples of alternative skill development for the on the stomach baby.

Sitting

Around the middle of the first year of life the baby begins to enjoy the world from a more upright position. Several important behaviors begin to emerge.

- Beginning to sit with little support;
- Rolling over, first from on the stomach to the back and then from on the back to the stomach;
- On body contact has occurred and reaching off body to sound is emerging or may have already occurred;
- Reaching out with hands to get objects touching the body first and then reaching for objects near the body; and
- Once the baby is sitting without support and has the range of behavior to freely move in this position, for example, rotate at waist, bend forward to pick up objects on the floor, and maintain balance if falling backwards, then the baby begins to go to a kneeling, four-point position (two hands and knees on floor).

These listed behaviors are just a few of the many activities the baby will be doing. What is important to remember is twofold. First, the quality of the baby's sitting will depend upon the components of movement and balance developed previously for this position. Second, the quality of the sitting will depend on the quality of the components of movement developed *before* sitting in the on the back and on the stomach positions. If the blind baby is missing one or more of the movement components when entering the sitting position, the quality of sitting will be compromised. Here we come to understand what the problem *truly* is, not blindness but a component or components of movement that can be addressed and most likely developed.

Babies will develop a better quality of sitting by being in their parent's lap or sitting between or alongside their parent's legs. In this way moving with and as part of their parent gives the babies a model of "felt" movement to observe. Chapter 5 gives examples of alternative skills to be used in facilitating the quality of movement in the sitting position.

Crawling

Around 9 months of age the baby can crawl or begin to crawl, experimenting on hands and knees (four-point position) moving backward and forward. It is natural for babies to move backwards when crawling initially and then forwards. It has been reported that blind babies, however, prefer to crawl backwards, perhaps because they are less vulnerable to hitting their heads. There is a great deal of variation in crawling with sighted babies. Some crawl for a very long time and then walk. Some, on the other hand, crawl very little, learn to walk and then go back to crawling. The point is this: *when sighted babies show a variation in a motor skill or components of movement we are not likely to think that sight is the reason for such behavioral differences. But when blind babies show the same variation we often will reference blindness as the cause. This does no service to the blind child who may need attention in working on what may be the "real problem" (if it is a problem at all) and that is the movement components required to accomplish a particular motor skill.*

During this time of learning to crawl and exploring the floor on all fours, the baby will discover any steps that are in the home. It is an important skill for all babies to learn to explore and eventually go up and down steps. Blind children are often kept away from steps at a developmentally appropriate time when they should be exploring them. Fear of falling and getting hurt is an understandable reason for keeping children away from the steps, but they need to learn the "ups and downs" of steps, where they lead, the boundaries at the sides, what they are composed of, and what covers them. There is another reason why it is important for blind babies to explore steps when they discover them. Many of the same components of movement that are used in crawling are also used to go up and down steps. Therefore, the blind baby that is delayed in crawling may benefit greatly through the exploration of steps.

Parents and professional service providers could put a few toys on a step for the child to explore or use their voice and/or the sound of a toy to invite the child to explore the next step up, down or sideways. The echo sounds on steps are usually interesting. And lastly, stairs introduce the child to "going someplace"—to bed, to take a bath, outside to play, or down to the basement. Steps are a natural transition to another activity. Make exploring steps a part of the crawling experience, getting to know what floor space can be, where it can lead and what it can do. The world is not comprised of one flat uncluttered surface but rather one that is uneven, has different textured surfaces, has inclines and declines, spaces that go up and down, and objects to be circumvented or checked out. Introduce the blind child to a variety of surfaces for exploration and this will facilitate the development of the components of movement when crawling.

Walking

When blind children are learning to walk they need postural security in this upright position. There is no freedom of movement for walking without balance. The quality of the components of movement and balance the blind child brings to walking will determine the ease or difficulty in mastering this skill. Many blind children walk without support with ease and confidence. Some blind children take months to move forward on their own once they have attained the standing position. The common assumption is that "fear of not seeing" is the reason for the delay in moving forward. This is a classic example of sighted bias, the thought of losing sight, at work here in this reasoning. *There are a number of factors that can come into play when the child has reached the point of being able to stand and is delayed in initiating walking. None of them have to do with blindness. Here are some reasons why.*

- The child has missed a number of components of movement and does not have the neurological or developmental readiness to take the first steps. For example, the child may not be able to coordinate the components of movement or has not developed adequate weight bearing and shifting, trunk rotation or reciprocal movement required in crawling.
- The child may not have experienced enough information about the ground, different textures, and uneven surfaces in prior motor experiences. Therefore, the child lacks the appropriate experience with body parts that are now expected to perform balance and coordination with only the two feet. This often occurs when blind babies have been carried too much beyond what is age/stage appropriate, and are not permitted or encouraged to experience the floor or ground surfaces.

  Many times, for fear of the blind child being delayed, or not walking within the "normal" time frame, parents will do a lot of walking with holding on to the child's hand before their child is ready for this position. Blind children *need to know "floorness"* in *all of the motor milestones before they can be expected to make sense out of floorness with just two feet. Being accustomed to the parent's hand, it is only natural that they do not want to let go of the perceived balance and control that holding on provides.*

- The blind child did not learn to pull to stand and cruise along furniture and walls. These experiences are needed to develop the experience base for confident walking. Balance is affected by more than neurological or motor factors; it has an emotional component too—the feelings of trust, security, and confidence in performing the movement. Such a feeling can be developed by independent standing and cruising.

All babies, when they learn to walk, like to carry something in their hand(s). This is one way of finding security. Some babies will hold their clothes, a stuffed animal, or a wooden spoon, for example. Blind babies are no different. They like to hold objects too. For years I thought that the cane should not be introduced to the blind child until after walking. Then an experience convinced me to change. I was working with a very developmentally delayed boy of about four years of age. He had been cruising for weeks, holding onto walls, furniture, and the hands of adults but he would not take steps in open space on his own. A week or two after holding a cane, he took his first steps into open space holding onto the cane without holding on to anyone's hand.

Why did it take me so long to think that if children liked to hold onto an object when learning to walk that the cane might be the most natural object to try with a blind child? The answer was my limited experiences to understand about the purpose and functioning possibilities of the cane, particularly with a multiple disabled blind child. The cane has a wealth of possibilities for blind children, including ones with additional disabilities. Chapter 4 on cane travel discusses many of these possibilities.

PROGRESSIONS IN THE DEVELOPMENT OF ECHOLOCATION

Echolocation is the utilization of the presence or absence of reflected sound to locate objects before making physical contact. An increase in frequency of sound waves is produced as an object is approached and a decrease in frequency of sound waves occurs when moving away from an object. So as the child approaches the object, the change in the frequency of reflected sound can be perceived. With time, the child can distinguish between objects in front, to the side and overhead. Blind people have described echolocation as a "felt sense of closeness," "pressure," "sound shadow," and "tunnel or sea-shell effect."

Through movement the child perceives subtle changes in the reflected sound and the resonance can be used in developing a plan for movement in a particular environment. For example, a crawling blind child may approach a wall, stop and sit down or may turn away to crawl in another direction. If the goal is to find the wall, the child reaches out to locate it. *This demonstrates the child's creative problem solving ability: the child observes its own actions through active movement and improves upon them to make them more efficient. The use of echolocation makes more out of what the environment is offering and attests to the fact that the blind child is a creator and experimenter, as are all children.*

In the developmental progressions outlined in this chapter, an awareness of the blind child's image and the environment does take place, although at times in different ways from a sighted child. Does this mean blind children think differently or that the *process of learning* is different?

No! What it does mean is that blind children may acquire information differently and the information they receive and perceive may be used differently than their sighted peers. Echolocation is an example of the blind child using the sound space world differently than the sighted child. This is an illustration that "differences aren't deficits." There are alternative approaches to human behavior and getting a job done.

In the exploration of the sound space world, blind children use hearing as a spontaneous means of exploring "auditory space." We know that children seek efficient strategies naturally and the greater efficiency in movement when using the sound space world would ensure that they would use it if they could. As adults, we are able to observe an increased quality to the movement of blind children and familiarity with their environment. It should be noted that sighted adults who have acquired blindness (adventitiously blinded) develop this ability as well. In my experience in working with blind adults it would seem that most develop this ability (to varying degrees) within the first year of becoming blind, especially if they have been introduced to using the cane.

Over the years the research has referred to this phenomenon as "object perception," "facial vision," and "echolocation." I prefer using the term echolocation with parents and children because it is an easy, vivid, tangible description for a process that is truly more complex than the term would indicate. When blind children use echolocation they are using more than reflected sound. It is about using primarily hearing, although there is some research to indicate the use of the "feeling of pressure" on the face to plan a different movement to avoid objects. Echolocation involves the location of objects far and near, such as a building across the street or an intersection of two hallways. It is about the understanding of this information and how it is *perceived* in making a plan for more efficient movement and travel.

Blind babies start very early to use and demonstrate echolocation in their movement. O&M specialists can be catalysts to facilitating this use of the sound space world by their direct involvement with the blind child and educating parents about echolocation. The more parents understand the nature of their child's ability to use echolocation, the more they will be able to nurture this skill development in their child.

Nurturing Echolocation

If we are to engage with blind children to assist the development of echolocation, it helps our understanding to think of it less as an isolated skill and more as part of the creation of purposeful thought and movement. The parent and O&M specialist can structure activities that will afford opportunities for the child to experiment. New possibilities can be created that will engender in blind children different ways of perceiving and thinking about the sound space world.

Sounds created in curious play and self-amusement are part of the exploration of the sound space world. In my own work with blind babies I have use different sized containers rich in resonance. I have experimented with other resonance spaces such as large cardboard boxes, tunnels (for example, one created by a tunnel-barrel-drum), plastic and metal cups, and pots and pans. Dr. Lilli Nielsen's Little Room and Resonance Board activities are excellent examples of resonance play spaces.

As the blind child grows and begins using the cane, echolocation will be expressed in a more advanced manner. Objects in the environment, such as walls, parked cars, and trees can be "heard." In this way the child is developing a greater sense of knowledge about the environment.

This also develops greater skill proficiency and autonomy in traveling about the world. *How can we expect the child to come to know the power of such abilities if we do not promote such potential?* Often what is promoted with blind children is their residual vision at the expense of not promoting other potentialities, like echolocation. Therefore, let's take a look at how echolocation can be expressed in the early years and how we might join in the process to promote its development.

The In-the-Arms-on-the-Floor Baby

During the early years parents are getting to know their baby through "touch affections." Blind babies give meaning to sounds through these pleasurable and secure touch feelings. The connection of loving touch and sounds become anticipated. Sounds will become more meaningful and will become the motivation for reaching to the object producing the sound. Eventually, the blind child reaches for an object without a sound or touch clue.

We may think of this as the equivalent of a sighted child reaching for an object hidden from view. Such a search without the use of vision has been cited as an example of object permanence. This aspect of the child's development is important, as it would take place *around the event* of the establishment of echolocation. As children pay increasing attention to the sound space world, they begin to understand touch, sound, and objects more meaningfully and then begin to discriminate, experiment with, and utilize more subtle sounds.

By choosing toys and activities rich in resonance we can introduce blind babies to an amusing sound space world. No one has contributed more to our understanding of resonance play space materials and activities than Dr. Lilli Nielsen. Her work has greatly contributed to our understanding of echolocation and how it can be nurtured in children under 3 years of age. By facilitating the connection of sound to touch, we can promote the development of auditory reach and echolocation in blind babies. One example of what a play sequence can look like is described below. Start by holding the open end of a plastic container or coffee can facing the child. It should be a few inches away from the child. Then:

1. Tap the bottom of a container. Child will reach for the sound with your verbal or tactile prompt.
2. Tap the bottom of container until child reaches for the sound without your verbal or tactile prompt.
3. Hold the container and slowly move it away and back again. The child will reach as a result of echolocation.

Some babies respond to step 3 without step 1 and 2 if they have clearly established the use of echolocation.

Blind babies demonstrate echolocation *after they learn auditory reach, using hearing to localize the sound of an object and reach for it. If the baby has not learned to reach off body to a sound object then the baby is less likely to reach towards a more subtle form of sound, as is the sound produced by echolocation.* Most blind babies will enjoy this activity. If the baby does not perform the task this could be due to several reasons: lack of interest at the time, unfamiliarity with the play situation, or interest in something else. This activity is not a test; rather, it is a suggested game for both parent and child to play with the beginnings of echolocation. Photos in chapter 5 give additional examples of using echolocation.

The Crawling Child

Echolocation expresses itself more obviously during the locomotion of very young blind children, especially around the event of crawling. As a consequence of observing and experimenting with echoes, self-protection, and more efficient movement in space is facilitated. For example, the baby may crawl up to a wall and hit its head. In an attempt to avoid hitting the wall the baby will demonstrate stopping and/or turning away from the wall. This is a self-protective behavior the baby has developed. Blind babies do this without any instruction in the use of echolocation. The sequence of events around the time of crawling that leads to such an effective use of echolocation may be described as follows:

1. Auditory reach off the body has taken place.
2. Change in sound frequency is perceived as a wall is approached or receded from; the child may slap its hand on the floor while approaching, playing with the sound, but still bump into the wall.
3. Knowledge that a specific object exists; the child reaches for the wall without touch, sound, or verbal prompts made by adults. The child touches the wall to validate the sense of anticipating it.
4. Change in sound "heard" is linked to the location of the wall; the child avoids bumping into it without touching it. The child may demonstrate slowing up, stopping or turning away from wall as it is approached.
5. Coordination of body movements with perception of reflected sound occurs; the child goes around or avoids the wall to get to another destination. For example, to get to the living room, the child crawls to the wall, does not bump into it, makes a left turn, goes to the end of the wall and turns into the room.

We can facilitate the use of echolocation by "coacting" with blind children, placing ourselves over the children while making crawling movements and slapping the floor to elicit their imitation. If it seems obtrusive to the children then don't do it. Because imitation is one way all children learn, we usually find the blind children making slapping sounds too. Rolling metal coffee cans makes wonderful sounds blind children enjoy hearing, locating, and chasing around the kitchen floor. (Be sure to cover any sharp edges of the can with tape!) These sounds produce echoes, resonance and vibration. This gives information about the boundaries of the world around the child. If the floor is laid on plywood it will be a natural resonance board, giving off reflected sounds that can be heard and played with by the child. The child is being amused and is acting on the world.

The Walking Child

As a new walker, the blind baby may appear not to use echolocation and may actually bump into the very wall that was avoided while crawling. The child still possesses the idea in the mind but may not be able to use it, as the event of walking may take full priority of concentration, reducing the attention the child is able to give to incoming sound information. As the child develops better balance and experience in walking, echolocation will be reestablished.

The same process of seeming to lose and then regain echolocation will take place outdoors. When the blind child is learning about different textures and uneven ground surfaces, less attention is given to the subtle reflected sounds. When the child is familiar and confident in moving in the outdoor environment, the use of echolocation will be reestablished.

The Cane Traveler

The cane is a tool that facilitates movement. It connects, protects, detects, informs, explores, and makes for more efficient travel. As the blind child learns to use the cane the same process we observe in learning to walk will occur; namely, the child will seem to lose and then regain echolocation. Once the child starts developing more purposeful movements with the cane, tapping it to explore the interesting sounds of the environment will begin. The child will learn to identify when a wall or a parked car (with the engine off) is near by tapping the cane. Gradually the typical blind child will be able to detect telephone poles to the side when walking on a sidewalk. Use of the cane for echolocation is discussed further in chapter 4.

The Exploring Child

As the blind child explores the world and integrates echolocation into more subconscious, automatic thought, more efficient behavior will be manifested. For example, blind children use their hands to explore the world of objects. This is part of the bottom-up process. When children are looking at a line of objects, as along a wall, or the wall itself, a sequence of behaviors I have observed as they are learning to check out "wallness" from the bottom-up is as follows:

1. The blind child faces the wall and scans (looks) with two hands on its surface. The leading hand gives preview and some protection. The other hand may be giving review of what was just experienced with the leading hand. I refer to this as a preview/review process.
2. As the blind child becomes more familiar and secure with this surrounding (previously scanned surface) there will be a natural and gradual switch to one-handed scanning. The child is then positioned more parallel to the wall.

3. Once the surface is "known" and the child is familiar with its characteristics, the child moves from the wall and becomes more parallel to it. The child will walk for an increasingly greater distance not touching the wall. Instead the wall is "heard" and is "known" to be there. The cane traveler gets more precise information than the child who is not using a cane.

4. Gradually the child is comfortable with "middle of hallway" walking, as the walls on both sides can heard through echolocation.

It should be noted that the conventional approach refers to following a wall as "trailing." As a result of discussing this with a parent of a blind child years ago, I decided to refer to this as "scanning." Trailing implies "lagging behind," whereas scanning suggests "looking" at the wall and learning about "wallness." Scanning seemed a more neutral and positive term. Using scanning to learn about walls, corners, and a straight line of objects from the bottom-up is not for the purpose of travel as in conventional trailing. Instead it is about sensory experiences leading to conceptual understanding of the environment.

So what we observe is the blind child going from two hands, to one hand and finally no hands, using echolocation. When using the cane, the blind child's behavior becomes even more efficient, walking in the middle of the hallway and checking the wall from time to time for the purpose of locating an object or destination. Blind children have been observed to self-initiate this sequence without instruction. *There are the techniques we teach children and there are those they teach themselves from the bottom-up.*

If we share in the blind child's developing awareness of echolocation, from infant to cane traveler, we will be part of the developmental process of independent movement and travel. We will be facilitating the efficiency and proficiency of a very important *blindness skill*. We will assist blind children in getting to know and move in the world in a more safe and effective manner. It is particularly important that the blind child becomes aware of this ability so it can voluntarily be used at will. The blind child's manifestation of echolocation is an example of a developmental process that, when nurtured, promotes independent movement and travel.

The alternative skills discussed in the developmental progression of echolocation is an example of how we adults can engage in the process of skill acquisition along with the child, as the child becomes an active mover and independent traveler. Echolocation is just one aspect of development utilized by the blind child. Hopefully this discussion pulled together the many topics in this chapter regarding progressions in the child's development. In this way a more vivid understanding of the main points discussed in the progressions of the child were mirrored in the development of echolocation. With our positive early intervention practices and interactions with the child, the different areas of child development integrate together to form a creative learner, active mover and independent traveler in the world.

CHAPTER 3

EARLY INTERVENTION, NOT EARLY INTERFERENCE

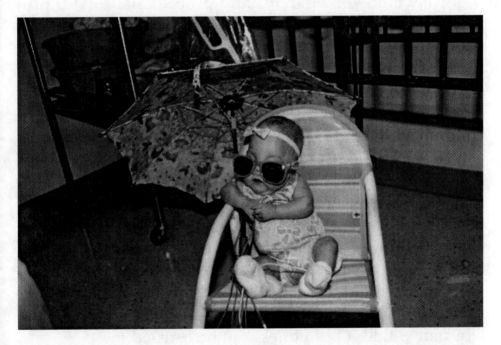

After being born severely premature and spending several months in the neonatal intensive care unit, this blind baby is now ready to come home from the hospital.

Independent Movement and Travel in Blind Children: A Promotion Model, pp. 93–141
Copyright © 2007 by Information Age Publishing

Fears are educated into us, and can, if we wish, be educated out.
—Karl A. Menninger

How blind children move and travel in the world will greatly depend on the care and intervention of parents and other educators. Adults exercise a great amount of control over the lives of children. The independent movement and travel of blind children can be facilitated and positively guided by parents and professional service providers. On the other hand, blind children are particularly vulnerable to adults making poor decisions about what they need and how they will learn.

The blind child is vulnerable by *nurture*, the "what" and "how" of our interventions and practices. There are blind children with typical child potential who do not develop as a typical child but are delayed in learning independent daily living skills. They are the result of a blindness system that has not delivered the opportunities and experiences to learn blindness skills at the appropriate age/stage. Their delays become misperceived as being caused by blindness. It is vital that parents receive reliable information about blindness utilizing a positive, typical child development standard for the blind child to which the alternative skills of blindness can be learned.

It is equally important that the same standard is used to guide parents and professional service providers to facilitate the independent movement and travel of blind children with additional developmental delays and/or disabilities. These children are vulnerable if the *nature* of the delay or disability or how to program for it is misunderstood. For example, severe premature birth, mental and emotional disorders, and cerebral palsy present complex problems that cause difficulties in organizing sensory information, compensating, and adapting. The causes of these developmental delays are *not* due to blindness. These children need additional intervention in the form of specialized treatment, educational approaches, and materials.

Dr. Lilli Nielsen's description of multiple disabled blind children as "especially developmentally threatened" is particularly useful in understanding their needs. Professional service providers with good intentions can, and at times do, interfere with the development of these children. In her book, *Are You Blind*, she presents thoughtful questions about what we do and how we do our interventions. The positive strategies of her Active Learning approach replace the deficit orientation of the conventional approach and offer the orientation and mobility (O&M) specialist new opportunities for understanding the promotion of independent movement and travel in these blind multiple disabled children.

This chapter discusses a number of concerns and issues of early intervention for blind children, with typical or atypical developmental abilities, that impact independent movement and travel. It is hoped that the positive interventions discussed in this chapter will reduce interference with developing the child's abilities and potential.

AN OVERVIEW OF EARLY INTERVENTION AND PRESCHOOL PROGRAMS

In the life of a blind baby, parents are introduced to programs and services to assist them caring for their baby's needs. Parents may have blindness professionals visiting the home and/or be involved in an early intervention program. This early intervention program can be home and/or center based. At 3 years of age generic disabled preschool programs become available to the blind child by school districts. The intent of these early intervention and preschool programs is to inform the parent about blindness and give direct intervention to the child. The professionals of these programs guide parents with suggested strategies, activities, and materials that are *intended* to facilitate the child's learning.

Over the years I have visited many of these early intervention and preschool programs and have met many dedicated hardworking professionals and learned much about development of the "typical child" by observing their work. More often than not, however, programs in early intervention and preschool know about the variety of developmental delays of sighted children but *not* about the blind child. They are *information poor* about blindness. Most of these programs have never been visited by an O&M specialist. The staff in these programs may know about independent movement and travel from an adult-centered point of view offered by conventional O&M. Some programs do have access to O&M professionals but even then the approach may not be from a bottom-up, developmental perspective.

There are some early intervention and preschool programs specializing in blindness for this young population. For those that have an O&M specialist on staff, this professional usually has not been exposed to early childhood courses that address independent movement and travel with babies or preschoolers. The profession does not have a specialization or certification in early childhood O&M. Some O&M professionals, like myself, have pieced together infant studies courses and early childhood courses and integrated the information learned from them into our work with young blind children.

There are progressive early intervention and preschool programs for blind children that do offer the skills of blindness. For example, they have Braille and canes for the children to experiment with and learn. The staff has incorporated a bottom-up perspective promoting the independent movement and travel of blind children. Such programs incorporate parents into programming so that they do not feel that someone else, namely the professionals, will do for their baby what they could not do.

Parents do what they do in raising their child 24 hours a day. They have a longer, more sustained and intimate relationship with their child than professional service providers. Yet, when they enter the kind of early intervention and preschool programs that present them with an attitude that implies "we know what is best for your child," parents are less likely to develop confidence in relating to and guiding their blind child. These professionals whose view is "from a distance" and who often are not on solid ground about their own knowledge base about blindness and specifically a developmental, bottom-up perspective in O&M, not only misguide the parent but the blind child as well.

In the early relationships of parent and child, they are "one unit" and over time the space increases into separate identities. The child grows on the nurture of the parent. If parents are guided with reliable and useful information about blindness, which includes a skill oriented "can do" approach, their child will assimilate this positive guidance into its own need to know and drive to move. Therefore, O&M professionals and other professional service providers in early intervention and preschool programs who respect the parent-child relationship will include the parent in all aspects of their programming.

PRACTICES IN EARLY INTERVENTION THAT PROMOTE INDEPENDENT MOVEMENT AND TRAVEL

Early intervention programs can offer opportunities for advancing the attunement between parents and their baby. Practices in early intervention can promote the independent movement and travel of the baby. Unfortunately, there are times when standard practices can interfere more than intervene on behalf of the child. A discussion of some of the standard practices with a highlight of how they can be an advantage for the blind child is discussed below.

Circle Time

Blind babies relate better in two-person or three-person groups. In such a small group blind babies can hear and touch others more readily than in a large group, and therefore, can relate more meaningfully to the adults in the small grouping. Circle time is usually part of the program where, as a large group activity, everyone sits in a circle and sings or shares conversation. Singing the "wheels on the bus go round and round" may be enjoyable for the staff but such circle time can be very irrelevant, confusing, and boring to the blind baby.

When observing these babies and their frustrated behaviors in large circle groups, it becomes obvious that something is wrong. Unfortunately, the common perception is that the blind child needs exposure to this type of setting and over time the "fussing" will diminish. Even if the blind baby's fussing diminishes, it does not mean anything positive has been learned about the group experience. Usually what has been learned is how to withdraw and go "inward" with the confusing information presented in such a large grouping. *Compliance should not be interpreted as developmental growth.*

The blind baby's sound information in a small group gives the opportunity to be validated by touching the persons in that group. In addition, the small group offers the intimacy of face-to-face experiences that the large group does not offer. Remember that in early development two senses go together to validate the experience and to synchronize the event for the baby. It is a more natural experience for the blind baby to participate in a small group where touch and sound possibilities can provide a more meaningful experience.

Exploring Time Versus Sit Down Time

Blind babies need to be exploring the environment, moving about and meeting their need to know and drive to move at their developmental level. Whether rolling over, scooting around on their bottom, crawling, or walking, blind babies must be permitted the opportunity to explore and discover. During the developmental period of time blind babies are in the early intervention program, they are at the "visiting the world" stage. They need to move and find out what is in their world and how to move among the people and objects in it.

However, much time is often spent in the program sitting down, circle time, snack time, doing fine motor, and other table tasks. During this time blind babies are not involved in locomotion to explore and visit their world. The sighted baby can observe the environment visually. The blind baby needs to move about and touch the object world to observe. I have often seen blind toddlers who are just beginning to explore their world walking about only to be seated and persuaded to take direction for adult guided activities at the table. Many demands are placed on these babies to perform. In general, does the typical parent of the sighted baby or larger society expect so much sitting down time and paying attention from the typical toddler?

Therefore, facilitate the standing upright toddler experience of walking about and exploring the environment. Remember, the concepts of familiarization before orientation, sensory before conceptual and meeting the need to know and drive to move are important to development. Early intervention is not preschool. Under 3 years of age, the child is still a baby. Whereas the sighted baby can get visual preview, the blind baby uses touch to explore, preview the environment, and map out the world.

Facilitating Therapies

In early intervention programs the blind baby often receives a variety of therapies, physical, occupational, and speech and language to name a few. A skilled therapist who knows child development and movement can be a very positive influence on the development of a child with delays and/or disabilities. Parents have the opportunity to facilitate independent movement all throughout the day of the child. Blind babies who receive therapy for a delay in development benefit when their parents observe the therapy session. In this way parents are able to facilitate the goals of therapy.

What goes on in therapy is often limited to the therapist's scheduled time with the child, and the parent is often not included. For example, the parent may be in a support group with other parents at the early intervention center at the same time as the child is in therapy. The results of therapy will be limited unless the therapist shows the parent how to employ the therapy practices into day-to-day living. Therapists who teach the parent promote confidence in the parent being the first and primary educator of their child.

Intended or not, there is often a felt urgency by the parent to get as much therapy as possible to "fix" the blind child. Where does this idea come from? From my point of view, delays are usually blamed on blindness and accepted as a given. Also, the parent is relieved to know that the delay is "normal." This perception, however, lowers expectations of engaging the parent in a more positive activity of alternative approaches and skills to be learned. Therefore, parents rely on the therapy to fix the perceived blindness delay and are not usually taught to perceive their role as essential educators in the process of developing new, alternative skills of blindness.

The Goal is Sensory Integration, Not Sensory Disintegration

One of the goals of early intervention programs is for children to learn to use their senses to be amused, explore, gather information and learn about their world. Sensory integration is the act of processing and incorporating this information into the child's personality. The hands of blind children are their eyes. They are the perceptual organs for the process of sensory integration. When the active movement of blind children is facilitated to explore the world with their hands, the need to know is being satisfied.

In early intervention, active movement is promoted when babies initiate, sustain, monitor, and terminate an activity with the use of their *own* hands. We can encourage babies to reach out and explore with their hands by introducing interesting sound and touch objects into their play space that they can pick up, explore, or mimic the sounds heard or create new sounds and touch experiences. We can set the stage in a type of environment we want the child to explore.

We must be mindful of our handling of the baby without the baby's permission or understanding. In early intervention programs a number of "hands on" the blind baby takes place. Each pair of hands touches and moves differently, conveying different messages to the child. This is often confusing to the blind child and results in more passive responses. It may be that there are too many hands on the child. *The goal of many forms of therapy and activities in early intervention programming is "sensory integration," but many blind children with the many hands on them and the resulting performance pressure end up with "sensory disintegration."* They withdraw and resist and other behavior problems are often created.

As in circle time, the common perception by professional service providers is that the blind baby needs exposure to other people and must learn to interact with others. Babies, however, do not always invite adults to touch them. Sighted babies can see the adult, perhaps a smiling face approaching them before they are picked up and handled. Even with this preview, many sighted babies do not like the interaction, especially if they are going through the stranger anxiety stage of development. Blind babies go through this stage too, plus the added factor of lack of visual preview. It is understandable, then, that the goal of sensory integration may not be achieved.

The parent of the baby is the most natural and first resource to know what the baby can handle regarding touch interactions. Asking parents for permission to hold or interact with their baby is the first step. When I made house visits regarding O&M consults, I would never spontaneously pick up a baby until after first observing the baby for a time and getting the parent's permission. Even then, I would rather model my suggestions through the parent's interactions with the baby and not my own handling of the baby.

Play

It is important to remember that a large part of a baby's wake time is considered playtime. Parents and professional service providers would be serving the child's best interest to place their energies on setting up the environment so that the blind child could self-initiate play and be self-amused. We want blind babies to move and self-regulate their own observation of the activity.

Play is the child's form of work in getting a job done. I remember visiting an early intervention program during the time when the activity was learning to go up and down a little indoor slide. The four toddlers in the group sat in chairs as, one at a time, each took a turn going up and down the slide. All the children in the group but one was watching the other children perform this fun activity. This was a blind child who, of course, could not see what was going on at the slide. Each time she got up to move over to the slide to check out the action, the teacher told the child to go back to her seat and that it was not her turn. The child was beginning to get frustrated because she wanted the same opportunity as the sighted children—to *observe* what was going on. I suggested she be able to stand by the slide and observe through touch and sound each child climbing up and sliding down. The staff tried this idea and it worked beautifully.

This suggestion is the most obvious thing if you are aware that this is the way blind children will get observation and an equal opportunity, as their sighted peers have, to observe. When there is a lack of awareness of how blind children will observe, then they are vulnerable to having their play experiences restricted. This results in active movement and active play being underdeveloped and negatively affects the spontaneity of the children.

The play of the child expresses the curiosity, organizing abilities, and imitation of others by observing them. Blind children observe others best by meaningful integration of touch and sound information, performing active movement, and exploration of the environment. Playing with the blind child, sharing the child's space and inviting the child to interact is more productive than having the child just sit and listen to others. For example, waiting for a turn is certainly a skill to be learned, but what toddlers are ready to learn this skill before they have experiences and enjoyment with the activity itself?

Introduction to Cane Travel

Early intervention programs promote independent movement and travel when they introduce the cane to blind children. This is best done with the parent's involvement. Many blind children begin using the cane with enthusiasm from around 1 to 3 years of age. The youngest child I ever gave a cane to for the purpose of walking was 11 months of age. I have introduced the cane with the pre-walker for a reaching out and exploratory tool when sitting before 11 months. Because the cane is a hand-held tool used by the child as a mover and traveler, it is not uncommon that physical and occupational therapists take an interest in the blind child using a cane.

Although the occupational therapist is concerned with hand skills and the upper part of the body and the physical therapist is primarily concerned with the lower part of the body, both work in a holistic manner with the early intervention population. Their roles can truly facilitate movement and travel skills with the cane and can contribute to a positive introduction, along with the O&M professional and the parent, to the child learning about the cane for the first time. Chapter 4 discusses an early, appropriate start to cane travel.

Because O&M professional service providers are not always available to consult with the early intervention or preschool program, therapists and other staff of these programs are usually reluctant to get a cane and initiate exploration experiences. The kind of alternative mobility devices that we can find in a typical early intervention or preschool program for other physically disabled children are often more involved and demand a greater amount of information regarding their use than the simple design and functioning of the cane. Do not let the lack of an O&M service provider limit your professional opportunities and responsibilities to the child.

Early intervention and preschool staff can be empowered by the parent of a blind child who may already have received information and, possibly, a cane for the child. Or they may learn from a published article or video about early cane use with blind children. Basic information is easy to come by, particularly from the organized blind who offer much information about the use of the cane with blind children. (See the Resources chapter for details on where to find such information.)

The information regarding O&M in this book invites you to get a cane and get started with the blind child during the early intervention years and preschool years. The concept of role release of information and permission to intervene, explore and practice with the child is being offered within the Promotion Model. Take the opportunity! It is the responsible, ethical and right thing to do!

PRESCHOOL IS THE FORMAL INTRODUCTION TO INDEPENDENT MOVEMENT AND TRAVEL

Preschool is the first formal introduction to "school." This initial experience for blind children in school will set the stage for what is expected from them by their teachers and other school staff. With a Promotion Model understanding of O&M and the appropriate introduction and adequate instruction of the skills of blindness, this can be a wonderful time of learning and moving forward in the process of gaining independence.

Training in O&M is usually required for preschool staff. A partnered in-service by parents and the O&M professional can be very effective. I discovered this to be the case in my years of doing training with parents for preschool staff. Parents are delighted to talk about their child in an intimate way that professionals usually don't offer. Long term goals in O&M and short-term strategies to achieve these goals can be the topic of the training.

Most classroom teachers and aides do not know what to expect or how to encourage independence in movement and travel with blind children. Some educators learn very quickly and are able to facilitate this process. There are some educators, however, who resist new information that challenges the practices in *their* classroom. Other times the blindness professional consulting with the classroom teacher regarding O&M is not sure about how to proceed with this very young child. And often the parent is not sought out as a resource for what to do.

Sometimes the *informed* parent in O&M is put in the awkward position of having to educate the educators. As you can imagine, this often meets with negative attitudes because educators generally believe they know what there is to know about the group of children they are teaching. If the parent is uniformed about positive approaches in O&M, as well as the school staff, everyone will be sending mixed messages to the child, including the students in the class, on how the blind child should move about in the class and school.

In the event that there is an O&M specialist involved, the parent can not assume that the child's movement needs and abilities will be promoted in an age/stage appropriate way. The time spent with the O&M professional will meet the child's needs if the goal of instruction is age/stage appropriate independence in independent movement and travel.

In the typical development of the blind child, it is not uncommon for an O&M professional to work with a child during the preschool years and never introduce the cane. The readiness curriculum being used may not be designed to introduce the cane to the preschool blind child. The sighted/human guide may be promoted and a precane, an alternative mobility device, may be introduced instead of the cane.

Children who have additional delays are even more vulnerable to being guided and may not be introduced to any travel device at all. Even with children who may have an additional physical disability, the cane can be added to their other mobility devices that may be used. A blind child with balance problems, for example, can use a cane and a support cane. In the one hand the child can hold the support cane and in the other, the cane for travel. Physical therapists will consider a cane for the blind child in conjunction with the support device for a motor disability if they are given information on how to proceed with the skills to use the cane.

If you are a parent reading this book, hopefully the information provided within will contribute to your understanding of your child's O&M needs. *When blind children are not moving about and guided by their own self-monitored movement in an age/stage appropriate manner, then they are moving about with someone else's guidance. You will need to decide that it is in your child's best interest that independent movement and travel is a priority. It is that important an issue.*

Blind children will be learning in this early introduction to movement and travel in preschool about what is expected to achieve independence in moving about in the class and school. Attitudes about being an independent traveler emerge in the preschool years and follow the children in the years to come. Children will either learn to take responsibility for their own actions, movement and travel or rely on others to take the responsibility.

PRACTICES IN PRESCHOOL THAT PROMOTE INDEPENDENT MOVEMENT AND TRAVEL

Moving Independently With the Cane

The process of independent movement and travel is in the "self-initiated" action. The typical blind child can be introduced to the cane before preschool and bring it to the first day of class. Introducing the cane works best when it is initiated at the home and early intervention and then transitioned to the preschool. This initiates the positive attitude that the blind child will be using the cane to move about at home and school.

The reality is that most blind children will not enter preschool with a cane. In this case, in the typical development of the blind child, it is *vital* that the child be introduced to and begin using the cane in the first year at preschool. For children who are blind and have developmental delays this should generally not stop them from starting with a cane if their developmental level is one year and older.

When blind children are introduced to the cane during early intervention or preschool, by the time they enter kindergarten they are ready for age/stage appropriate movement and travel with their peers. They will have a few years of learning to experiment and practice with the cane; home and school will be familiar and supportive of its use and the initial elementary school transition will be a smoother and more positive experience for everyone.

Economical Use of the Sighted/Human Guide

The common practice suggested by conventionally trained professional service providers is for the child to get around using the sighted/human guide. With preschoolers the child may be guided by holding on to the

arm or forearm of the guide or just pairing off and walking hand in hand. Blind children who have a cane can
hold onto someone else with one hand and the cane with
the other. In one preschool class the teacher had the children hold onto a knotted rope. I had the blind child hold
the cane in the free hand.

It is understandable that all children in preschool are
getting to know the school and need to be monitored in
how they move in the class and in the hallways. Blind children, however, are more vulnerable than their sighted
peers to being excessively monitored and guided, especially when there is a specific technique named and taught
to them for this purpose. The guided technique often
becomes the *primary* way of getting around the school.
This method does not give practice for children to observe
their own movement; rather, they observe the movement
of others. This sets up a belief system that someone else is
the independent traveler and the child is the follower.

Please note the guided technique, as a chosen *option* by
children when they know how to get around the school (or
whatever environment), is at times a useful and sensible
choice for movement and travel. What the Promotion
Model opposes is when blind children, who have not yet
developed the orientation, movement, and travel skills
and confidence to move about independently, are taught
to have others guide their way.

This sighted/human guide technique is part of the precane, conventional O&M curriculum. It is taught as the
first skill to be learned, as soon as children begin to walk
and, as such, interferes and delays blind children developing age/stage appropriate independent movement and
travel skills. In being guided this way, how will blind children ever get the experience, practice, and confidence
base to move on their own in the world? If blind children
can only move about under the direction of a guide, then

they will not gain the personal freedom to go wherever and whenever they choose.

There is also the factor of safety. Would the child know how to exit the class and the school, for example, in a fire drill? All sighted children learn this in a fire drill. What we often observe in the fire drill with the blind child is the sighted/human guide. Even when the child has a cane for travel, it may have been left back in the classroom. There may come a time when there is a real fire and the blind child is separated from the guide or group. If children are without their cane they may be placed in harm's way. Blind children must learn to rely on their own resources, with proper instruction and age/stage appropriate goals.

Exploring Time

Exploring time to discover and learn about the environment can be built into the schedule of the blind child's school program. It is important for the blind child to experience the class and school that the child's sighted peers see as they walk to the class and move around the classroom. One activity for exploring time is the "cane walk." The blind child with the teacher or an instructional aide can learn about the objects that fill the classroom and the halls of the school. From the bottom-up, the child can learn about what fills the space in a school, just like the sighted child can see what objects occupy space. Exploring time is a purposeful use of school time to learn about and get full disclosure of what is in the school environment.

The O&M professional can give guidance on how to implement such a cane walk. I suggested to preschool teachers that the child be given perhaps 15 minutes a session, preschool usually being a half-day session and more time if the preschool was all day. During this time the child could find new objects, find out about what they do, and what they are called. Then the child could learn about where they are located and how to find the objects again. On any day of the week the child could always find new objects. For example, in the classroom it could be a chalk tray, the CD player, or a plant to be watered. In the hallway, objects such as a fire extinguisher, steps to a stage, or vending machine could be of interest.

Another example of exploring time is the use of a "choice box." Here the child chooses an object from several in a shoebox. Each object represents a part of the room. After the child chooses an object, the child must find the area of the room where that object belongs. In preschool, for example, a plastic cup and saucer would belong in the house area.

Over time, this familiarization with objects will develop into a working orientation of the classroom and the school. Familiarization before orientation is an important building block to include in the child's preschool exploration time.

Being a Line Leader

Walking in a line is such an important skill for children to learn in preschool that it is vital that blind children learn this skill too. Blind children need to learn to walk at the beginning, middle, and end of a line. All too often blind children learn to walk at the end of the line, usually verbally or physically guided by an instructional assistant. What they need to learn is how to keep up with the group on their own. Blind children must learn to walk in the middle of the line and to use their cane appropriately. And of course it is crucial, as it would be to any child, to learn to walk as the line leader. All children need practice to learn a skill. A blind child, if not given the opportunity to practice being a line leader, will never learn to accomplish such a skill and, more importantly, will come to believe that it is not possible to be a line leader.

If children are not using a cane but relying on partial sight, for example, then their sight must be efficient enough to stay in line without verbal or touch prompts. Children who need such prompts are not taking responsibility for their own movement. *The partially sighted child without a cane should be receiving no more information to walk independently than the typical sighted child is receiving. The partially sighted child that is being monitored more than sighted peers for movement and travel is in need of a cane.* Further information on the partially sighted child and cane travel is presented later in this chapter.

Essentially, whatever the sighted child needs to learn to move about safely and confidently during the preschool years is what the blind child needs to learn. The movement and travel skills that are dependent on vision can be learned by the blind child in an alternative way. The goal of O&M in the preschool years should be an age/stage appropriate taking of responsibility for independent movement and travel. Blind children can only do this if adequate instruction is given with the appropriate travel tool, and when the parents and school staff have been trained to facilitate the goals of independence in movement and travel.

CONSIDERATIONS FOR BLIND CHILDREN WITH DEVELOPMENTAL DELAYS

There are blind children who enter early intervention, preschool, and elementary school with developmental delays. Some have been diagnosed with additional disabilities. The disabilities may be physical, sensory, cognitive, or emotional and they may be mild, moderate, or severe.

These children may be in a generic special education pre-school class, one for a specific type of education classification or one for the multiple disabled. Whatever the reason for their developmental delay, these blind children have independent movement and travel needs too.

Below are several of these groups of blind children with delays/disabilities and considerations for their independent movement and travel.

Severe Prematurity

It is important that blind children entering preschool have an accurate adjustment for prematurity. I have presented the case for taking into consideration the months premature and the months in the hospital, adding those months together, and their total would be subtracted from the child's chronological age. This age would more accurately adjust for prematurity. For example, it would not be surprising to have a child entering preschool, who because of being born severely premature, was developmentally a toddler. Cognitively the child may be quite bright but the overall education program would need to factor in that not all areas of development may be on a 3-year-old level. Regarding O&M, these children will need a lot of active movement, exploration time, and practice learning to use their sensory information adequately.

For example, as babies, many of these preschoolers often underwent eye operations to "save sight" in the first 2 years of life. It would not be uncommon for these babies to experience a half dozen or more surgeries during this time. Such surgeries and their follow-up procedures are often obtrusive to developing the early components of movement, such as bringing the hands to midline; the baby's hands are pushed away from the face to avoid harm to the eyes while recovering from surgery. This delays the natural inclination of the baby to bring the hands in front of the face, toward the middle of the body. The babies are often described as "tactile defensive." It is no wonder many of these babies are defensive to being touched after being subjected to such medical interventions, not only to save sight but when they were also in the neonatal intensive care unit where they lived for months before they came home from the hospital.

If the blind preschooler born with severe prematurity demonstrates tactile defensiveness, one way to reduce the direct touch to the hand and yet give information about the environment when moving and traveling is with the cane. The cane allows the child to be in charge of what is being touched and explored. This is a much less invasive practice to contact the world than to take the child's hand to guide movement and exploration. In addition, all children are sensitive to having their bodies manipulated by others to perform activities that they can learn and want to initiate themselves. We are also living in a time of awareness of stranger danger. What do we teach blind children when they accept passively bodily manipulation by others in the everyday performance of tasks?

Consequently, if the parent and professional service provider have not promoted a more accurate understanding of the child's developmental needs, and the adjustment for prematurity has been dropped, the classroom teacher will be at risk for being misguided. The result could be teaching activities that are not at the developmental level of the child. Sometimes children are placed in a class that is below their cognitive ability because the adjustment for prematurity has been dropped and the inaccurate perception of the developmental level is so mismatched from the chronological age. If they are misplaced educationally, a life of misplaced perceptions about the children begins, based on misconceptions of the impact of severe prematurity and about blindness.

Additionally, it may be more appropriate to repeat a year in preschool or kindergarten than enter a grade that the child will be perceived as needing special placement, especially when this child may have spent the good part of the first year of life in the hospital. The extra year will reveal the true potential of the child, assuming the child has been given opportunity to learn the developmentally appropriate skills to succeed.

Additional Physical Disabilities

In Budapest, Hungary, there is a program called Conductive Education. It is a program for the disabled child with cognitive and/or physical disabilities, such as cerebral palsy or head trauma. The program's philosophy is "orthofunctional." This means the child learns by doing functional daily-living skills, which are considered essential and are valued along with academic learning. Regardless of age, before children can advance to their local schools in this program, they must learn to be mobile, handle their own needs in the bathroom and be able to feed themselves.

Conductive education asserts that through the child's own movement come opportunities for practice and development of *functional skills in the way the child can do them.* For example, greater emphasis is placed on the child getting to the classroom, even if it means getting there late, than for someone to assist the child to get there on time. This program is an excellent example for promoting the independent movement and travel of children with physical and/or cognitive disabilities.

Using this philosophy we can apply a "can do" approach to the child with additional disabilities learning to move and travel in a different way, as with wheel chair travelers. A blind child who uses a wheel chair would have greater possibilities for movement and travel with a one-wheel drive, motor-driven chair. With this type of chair only one hand is needed to operate it. This leaves the other hand free to hold a cane and clear the path of movement. This independence promoting set-up would be superior to someone else pushing the chair for the child, which is another form of guiding. It gives the child the opportunity to develop independence as a traveler. The cane would need to be long enough to reach over the curb and touch the street and detect other drop-offs in the environment. The next chapter deals with the longer cane approach to travel, which would be needed for a child in a wheel chair. In Chapter Five there are photos and examples of blind children with physical disabilities using their canes.

Deaf-Blind

The deaf-blind child is someone with two sensory disabilities that combine to be considered for educational purposes as one combined disability. *These two disabilities, blindness and deafness, do not make a cognitive disability.* The use of the cane for deaf-blind children is essential for them to travel with safety and efficiency. The cane is a natural conductor and producer of resonance and vibration information. Such information is very useful to deaf-blind children. It will only be natural that deaf-blind children will rely on touch as their primary sensory system. The less in tact the child's vision and hearing, the more touch will be used and the more the cane will be relied on.

And yet in school programming these children are often misunderstood by their teachers who do not understand their dual needs. I was fortunate in my experience to work with a family that understood their deaf-blind child, were informed about his needs, and advocated for a "success curriculum" in school. This curriculum included Braille, cane travel, and visual and nonvisual techniques. The parents were informed about blindness and deafness, and provided training for the school staff and the professional service providers, like myself, in deaf-blindness. As a team we were able to promote the independence of their child.

Many programs for the deaf are not comfortable with educating a deaf-blind child because it requires a broader understanding of a range of skills. The skills used for the deaf child are visual and therefore don't work for a blind child. Even a deaf-blind child with considerable partial sight will need to learn nonvisual skills as well. The auditory skills used for the blind child do not work either. Therefore, many programs do not have resources that can guide them with the deaf-blind child. Once they understand that the blind child can learn alternative skills, like the deaf child learns for this disability, then a better understanding is reached regarding the dual *sensory* nature of the deaf-blind child.

It should be a common practice in teaching cane travel for the deaf-blind child to provide a cane that is rich in resonance and tactile feedback. Instead, it is more prevalent for a folding cane that has elastic down the shaft, which will dampen resonance and tactile feedback, to be given to the deaf-blind child. This type of cane should not be the cane of first choice for the deaf-blind child. When learning to use the cane, the deaf-blind child needs a cane that will afford superior resonance and tactile feedback. The characteristics of this type of cane will be covered in the next chapter.

Pervasive Developmental Disorders

There are a number of disorders that have a pervasive effect on children's ability to learn across all their developmental areas. This is not simply a cognitive disability but can affect the emotional and behavioral development of the child. One such pervasive developmental disorder is considered to be autism. There are different types of autism and different functioning levels of the child. Regardless of level of functioning, being totally blind or partially sighted, I have found that blind children with autism or another pervasive developmental disorder (PDD), need a specially designed curriculum for their condition. The resource I found to be the most useful as an O&M professional working with these children is Dr. Lilli Nielsen's *Are You Blind*. The Resources chapter gives more information about this book.

From my experience a few behaviors stand out with these children that I have learned to factor into their O&M program. One behavior that has an effect on teaching O&M is this: the way these children learn something for the first time is the way they want to continue to learn it. Now this does not seem so unusual as we humans like to continue to do things the way we learn them. What is different, however, with PDD children is that they will resist, sometimes with formidable adverse behavior, learning a new approach to a skill taught them, as in the use of the cane.

For example, I remember teaching a child with PDD who had developed reliable, basic cane skills. I wanted her to learn how to use the cane in the other hand as well, as there are times when cane travelers will need to switch hands, as in coming to a stairway if they hold the cane in the right hand and the railing is on the right. This child would rather go down the stairs not holding on or move over to hold the railing on the left. One day while doing the cane lesson with her, my shoe became untied and I asked her to hold my "teaching" cane (which I use to role model cane skills). As I bent down to tie my shoelace, she walked down the hall using both canes, as a child would use in "Double Dutch" jump rope.

As I looked at her using both canes with no difficulty, I had one of those "ah ha" moments. She was demonstrating the "add on" theory of teaching not the "taking away" approach. Each time I tried to get her to switch hands with her cane, she would not want to give up the cane from the right hand to the left hand. But in this case she didn't need to because she had two canes. So I started using two canes with her until she was comfortable and liked the feeling of using either hand and then she was able to switch hands spontaneously with little difficulty.

What are some of the instructional implications of working with children with PDD? First, the earlier you introduce a cane, the easier it is for these children to be more flexible to change and the easier it is to build on and alter cane skills. Second, using a cane with the same design, no matter what the length, is easier for children to learn more advanced skills than using a cane that changes in design as length increases. For example, one major manufacturer of a child's cane only goes up to 34-36 inches and when a longer cane is needed, the design of the cane changes. This could be a problem for PDD children to make a smooth adjustment to the new cane design. And third, never start with a precane device. Go directly to the cane. Children using alternative mobility devices have a more difficult time transitioning to the cane. More information about issues and concerns with precanes is given in the next chapter.

Cortical Visual Impairment

For the purpose of this chapter, many blind children who are developmentally delayed or multiple disabled, who have Cortical Visual Impairment (CVI), usually do not develop "functional" use of their vision until after the preschool years. CVI has been described as "blind sight." That is, the child's eyes may look, but the brain does not interpret what is seen and guide the child to act on what is seen. Now here's the good news. Research has shown that active movement on the part of the child triggers the visual cortex. This means that the avenue to developing whatever vision may be available in the CVI child is more likely to occur with a menu of active movement experiences.

The way to naturally develop vision is best done through active movement as opposed to the conventional approach of "vision stimulation activities." The conventional approach works with the weakest system (vision) and ignores, or does not utilize fully, the tactile/touch, movement, and auditory systems. The claimed success with the approach that uses the visual stimulation activities with the CVI child has to do with the child's response in a particular learning environment and is not necessarily generalized to other environments. Whether the child has truly integrated the use of vision into the personality and functionally or employs the vision spontaneously for everyday skills is another matter. CVI children are more likely to use functional vision when it becomes integrated into their personality. They can best learn this through independent movement experiences.

For example, let's say the goal is to have a CVI child visually track a ball through midline. It would make more sense to have the child move a ball on a table from one side to the other, rather than for the adult to hold the ball in front of the child, passing it though midline (side-to-side). Why do I think this to be so? When the child is moving the ball, the child is in control of the movement, using touch. The movement and the touch go together, a synchronized event. The child is more likely to trigger or register a visual response than an adult who is passing the same ball off the body of the child and through the visual field. The child's self-monitored experience is connected to its body. The adult's activity is not directed from the child's brain and is off the body and, therefore, is more removed from the child's experience. In the development of the child, touch and vision are integrated on body before off body.

Multiple Disabled

Multiple disabled blind children have delays in independent movement and travel for many reasons. Some of them are as follows:

- These children may not be able to process the information and therefore are not able to observe their own movement as the typical blind child.
- Due to cognitive delays, purposeful thought and movement develop more slowly. As a result, these children require much more practice with the components of movement. This will give them more opportunity to observe their own movement and to more adequately perform typical independent movement and travel skills.
- They often have delays in extracting clues from the environment and need much more practice with movement to get information from the environment that they can use for purposeful thought and movement.
- Maladaptive behaviors develop and delay the learning of developmentally appropriate skills. Often these behaviors are the result of the child's learning needs being misunderstood; children may become frustrated when they are forced to perform an activity they are incapable of doing or do not want to do.

Whatever the reason for the child's developmental delay, it is essential that professional service providers have a realistic understanding of the typical capability of the blind child, which is the same as any typical sighted child. If this is understood, more accurate placement and programming of the multiple disabled children will take place.

I am reminded of a child who has a pervasive developmental disorder, similar to autism. The parents were misguided into thinking his behavior was caused by the blindness. The preschool staff felt that they didn't know how to do work with a blind child. In truth the teacher *did* know how to teach a blind child, but not a blind child with autism. Once the strategies were in place to factor in this child's other educational needs, the typical skills of blindness did work and the child began progressing at a more appropriate rate of development.

The next section of this chapter will give more information regarding the multiple disabled children and the use of an Active Learning approach to facilitate independent movement and travel in blind children.

ACTIVE LEARNING CAN FACILITATE THE ROLE OF THE O&M PROFESSIONAL

Active Learning is an educational approach that diverges from conventional practices with multiple disabled blind children, particularly in its belief of "hands off" the child when teaching the child. This differs from the conventional practice of "hands on," when the adult is coacting with the child through touch interactions. This hands on practice is less obtrusive with the typical blind child who understands the interactions of the adults hands, but is more obtrusive for the child under 36 months of age with multiple disabilities who often does not understand or invite such touch interactions with adults.

Active Learning can offer an alternative to the conventional O&M approach for professionals working with multiple disabled blind children *developmentally* under 3 years of age. The Active Learning approach means being unobtrusively available to the blind child, respects the body space of the blind child and facilitates learning in a way that hand over hand does not. In the O&M professional service provider's role in facilitating and teaching echolocation and movement and travel skills with the cane, Active Learning can promote more successful outcomes. The child is learning in a way that employs unobtrusive availability, and elicits active movement from the child for more natural age/stage appropriate development.

For example, one approach developed by Dr. Lilli Nielsen is the use of the Resonance Board. O&M professionals can learn to make and use the Resonance Board, the details of which can be found in her books. It is made of a particular piece of wood framed in such a way as to conduct resonance. The adult and/or child can sit upon it and play with objects rich in resonance. The items chosen for the child to contact and interact with are the result of an assessment of the child's needs and level of development. Verbal feedback from the adult observer is given at strategic times that do not conflict with the child's own vocalizations or activity.

When the same objects are placed on a carpeted floor they would not offer the sound feedback that is offered by placement on the Resonance Board. A blind child listening to the sound space world often hear the sounds coming from a distance, echoing off the ceiling. By using the Resonance Board, the sounds come nearer to the child and are, in fact, "close at hand." This motivates the child to reach and explore, making the sounds happen again and again. Since repetition is a very important part of creating memory, the use of the Resonance Board facilitates such repetition and practice.

Another example is when teaching the cane to the blind child developmentally under 3 years of age. Whether developing as a typical or developmentally delayed child functioning below 36 months, the child will participate in interacting with the cane through exploring and experimenting with it. The parent can be very instrumental here because the child's mother or father would be the most natural person to introduce the cane. Because learning cane travel is a confidence-based skill, when the cane is first introduced at a young age, the child is more likely to have trust and confidence with the interactions of the parent than a professional service provider.

Active Learning is an educational approach to learning for multiple disabled blind children. The Resources chapter has more information on Dr. Nielsen's books. This very useful approach to teaching multiple disabled blind children can be of benefit and guidance to the O&M specialist. Those parents of blind children and professional service providers who have read and employed the strategies of Active Learning have met with success in facilitating independent movement and travel.

WHAT ACTIVE LEARNING AND THE PROMOTION MODEL HAVE IN COMMON

Active Learning and the Promotion Model both place an emphasis on what and how the child is learning and on how the child is being taught. When O&M professionals place more time and energy on the learning environment for the blind child, they are setting the stage for more positive outcomes. By educating parents and school staff on how to facilitate independent movement and travel, a team approach is created. This promotes the independent movement and travel in blind children from the bottom-up, rather than isolating the teaching of

O&M to just the one-on-one instruction time with the child. What's more:

- In working with children both use a "gain" approach and not an approach based on vision loss. They believe in skill development and integrating these skills into the personality of the child.
- Touch is the primary sense and self-initiated movement is the first requirement in getting to know and function in the world. The *brain is an equal opportunity employer* and does not discriminate in how it will get its information.
- The typical educational experiences of the blind child and multiple disabled blind child are in need of an alternative approach to understanding movement and travel needs. The conventional approach of "hands on" must become "hands off" when the child is at a developmental level that does not allow for comprehension of the adult's hands interacting with them. This means that the permission of the child is required for a "hands on" intervention.
- The child's entire range of skills is considered. The focus is functional *skill* assessment in all areas and not just functional *vision* assessment. Active Learning is targeting the multiple disabled blind child and O&M professionals are responsible to teach them as well as the typical developing blind child.
- Both agree that the blind, partially sighted child is often pushed to the point of inefficiency with the conventional "vision stimulation and training" approach. This causes a negative result in the child's self-esteem and delays the learning of more efficient skills.

In Chapter 5, there are several photos of learning environments developed by Dr. Nielsen. They are just a few examples of the many materials and learning environments that encompass Active Learning. The structure and function of the materials and environments afford the child an opportunity for active movement. In these environments children learn to self-initiate, sustain, monitor, and terminate their own movements.

A FEW OF THE PRINCIPLES OF ACTIVE LEARNING AND THE IMPLICATIONS FOR ORIENTATION AND MOBILITY PROGRAMMING

Many conventionally trained O&M professionals do not think they have much to offer the blind child *until the child is walking*. It is not unusual that they do not *perceive* their role to engage with the multiple disabled blind children who often have delays with walking and other areas of motor development. The Active Learning educational approach specializes in the development of multiple disabled blind children and has much to offer the prewalker. By becoming more familiar with the Active Learning approach, O&M professionals can create a greater involvement with the prewalking blind child. Below, I have outlined some considerations for O&M professionals, hopefully creating more of a comfort zone to engage with the multiple disabled blind population.

- The belief that the multiple disabled blind child is *teachable* permeates Active Learning and the Promotion Model. When professional service providers throw up their hands in frustration and say there is nothing more that they can do for *these* children, what they are really saying is there is nothing more that they *know how to do* with these children. We must offer an educational approach that *works for this popu lation.* Conventionally trained O&M professionals can learn to plan appropriate strategies and practices for multiple disabled blind children to facilitate independent movement and travel.

- The "teaching cane" (further developed in the next chapter) is one example of the adult's hands being placed less on the child. As children explore the cane the parent is holding and gradually take more and more interest in it, they will initiate more active movement. Self-initiating, sustaining. and guiding movement is the goal O&M specialists should be working toward with the blind child.

- Active Learning offers us many materials and ideas for creating environments that facilitate independent movement. Some of these are the Little Room, the Essef Board, Lap Board and Support Bench. What these materials have in common is that their structure and function are rich in affording active, self-initiated movements of the child. What does this say for the type of canes we O&M specialists provide the blind child? What are we to make of canes that are too heavy, dampen resonance and have reduced vibration and tactile feedback? The same care should be taken in deciding what cane to give the blind child, so that it affords opportunities for exploration and skill proficiency. In Chapter 5 are photos of other materials and practices from the Promotion Model that facilitate the child self-initiating action and moving independently.

- Dr. Nielsen sets down the sequence of learning a skill and breaks it down into steps, as evidenced by her book, *Early Learning, Step by Step*. For example, she describes the sequence of activities children must learn to use a tool, such as a spoon, to feed themselves.

In working with blind children, The Promotion Model takes a developmental approach, using alternative skills that are appropriate to each stage of development. There are progressions that take place in the early years that are not understood or taken in account in the conventional, adult-entered approach to O&M.

- Active Learning is very concerned that the intellectual level of the child should match the emotional level of the child for the selected activity. Accordingly, O&M should be developmental, and the task we give children to learn should be appropriate intellectually and emotionally. In the Promotion Model, I have given examples in previous discussions on the premature baby and the consequences for programming or working with the child with a pervasive developmental disorder (PDD).

- Blind children are often "done to" with too many hands on them. Active Learning refers to this approach as producing a "learned helplessness" on the part of blind children who become more passive as others do for them. In addition, multiple disabled blind children withdraw and do not want to perform the task. The Promotion Model asserts that active movement will be delayed when we adults promote, intended or not, the passive movement of blind children, particularly with the overuse of the sighted/human guide.

- Guiding hands *without permission* encourages a different strategy than the one the child is trying to develop. O&M specialists can be obtrusive to blind children developing their own search pattern by imposing the adult's style of what is considered the typical approach to learning a skill. Through the use of exploring and deciding where, when and how to move, without hands on intervention and unnecessary guiding, the blind children can develop their own strategies and style that works best for them.

- When using materials, the Active Learning approach utilizes two sets of materials, one for the child and one for the adult. In this way the adult can demonstrate without interfering with the child. In my own work with blind children I use my teaching cane and children have their cane. For example, I can tap the cane with a wider arc for better coverage and blind children can hear the difference and do the same with their cane. This is a very different approach than putting my hand on the child's hand and using tactile prompts to guide the hand of the child to perform a wider arc and tap of the cane.

- In Active Learning, if the child doesn't learn a task after trying a particular skill, then another approach is used. When we do not change our approach, Active Learning suggests that we have made a decision that the child is not teachable. By not changing our approach, the assumption being made is that the child can not learn in any other way. In O&M professional jargon this is put in a report as "lack of readiness," which means the blind child is not going to get O&M services or, if the child does get services, they will focus on precane skills and devices and not the cane.

Therefore, O&M service providers must be informed of the continuum of practices available to the blind child and be prepared to experiment with a variety of approaches. Incorporating the approach of Active Learning to promote independent movement and travel in multiple disabled blind children will result in very successful outcomes for independent movement and travel.

INCORPORATING ACTIVE LEARNING AND THE PROMOTION MODEL IN AN EDUCATIONAL ENVIRONMENT

When O&M specialists incorporate any of the above approaches and practices in their program of working with blind children, the challenge exists of introducing these ideas to a school that is not familiar with Active Learning or the Promotion Model. Through partnerships with parents, I have found success with doing the following:

- Both the parent and the O&M professional need to educate the teachers and staff. This can be done in a workshop for the school. If the Active Learning curriculum is being advocated, then teachers must learn the developmental assessment goals in the FIELA (**F**lexible, **I**ndividual, **E**nriched, **L**evel **A**ppropriate) curriculum. They must also understand the goals and instructional guide of the O&M professional. The school must become aware of the independent movement and travel of age/stage appropriate blind children. The "big picture" can be given by using videos, photos in this book and other published works. The Resources chapter gives information for ordering such materials.
- Active Learning goals need to be written into the IEP (individualized education program). Goals for independent movement and travel need to be written along with the instructional guide to achieve these goals.
- Materials must be supplied and/or shown where they can be ordered. The bottom-line is the school must have the materials. Some of these materials are costly and some are inexpensive. By training the school in the use and appropriateness of the materials, the

school district is more likely to buy into the cost effectiveness of the outcomes they will produce.

- The parent, O&M professional, and the school need to be working together for consistency between home and school on the Active Learning approach and Promotion Model goals, strategies, and practices for independent movement and travel.

It is hoped that this discussion of the Active Learning approach, as I understand it as a O&M specialist using the Promotion Model, gives you new ways of thinking about approaching independent movement and travel with blind children and especially the multiple disabled blind child.

SUCCEEDING WITH PARTIAL SIGHT: KEEP IT NATURAL AND USE ALTERNATIVE SKILLS OF BLINDNESS

The Promotion Model recognizes the following in order to more fully understand development in partially sighted children. First, the precursor to visual reach is tactile reach. That is, in typical development, visual reach does not come first. All babies learn to reach with touch before they learn to reach with vision. And second, the sensory systems are interconnected and develop simultaneously; the eye to see, the hand to reach, and ear-hand coordination. For example:

- Two hands come to midline around the same time as binocular vision occurs.
- Shift of visual gaze and tactile release of a hand-held object occur around the same time.
- Stimulation of one pupil creates a similar response in the other eye, or when the baby is in an asymmetrical

tonic neck reflex position ("fencing position") stimulation of one hand creates movement in the other hand.

- Random eye movements parallel the random movements of the hand, arm and leg.
- The eyes move more independently from the head and the hands move more independently from the arms around six months of age.

So what we observe in the child is an "interconnectedness" of the sensory systems and a simultaneous multisensory development of movement, reaching out, and getting to know the world.

Because the baby with "normal" vision does *not* have 20/20 vision at birth, what does this say for the visual efficiency of the partially sighted baby? Research has shown that at 2 weeks of age, babies with "normal" vision recognize and show preference for face-like patterns over random patterns. As professional service providers we understand what this implies for the totally blind child: we must offer an alternative menu of experiences to promote development. But we are less sure of what this information about early visual development implies for the partially sighted baby. If we insist on a vision first agenda of vision stimulation that tries to push partially sighted children to compete with only 10% or less of what their sighted peers are using to see, we are placing these children at a disadvantage and in harm's way.

The Promotion Model is more functionally oriented. Regarding the use of partial sight, it can be described as such: children have vision for what they can see and the skills of blindness for what they can't see. Such thinking is based upon what we know as the natural development of all children. For example, within the first days of life, the newborn brings its hands to its mouth, face, ears, nose, and eyes. This sequence is repeated over and over until further development of "on body" exploration develops. Such early on body contact is tactually directed and is the *precursor* to visual reach. Therefore, touch contact on body occurs before reaching off body for objects. When vision is verified by touch, this facilitates the learning of visual reach, on and then off body. This is the natural course of events in the developing child.

So why do we take an unnatural approach in the *vision first agenda* for the partially sighted child when we *first* require children to look with their partial vision to locate an object and then *reach* with their hand to pick it up? With multiple disabled, partially sighted blind children, vision may take even more time to integrate with other sensory information and be utilized. Therefore, more touch is needed. Auditory reach will also be delayed in multiple disabled blind children. Therefore, elicit visual responses through the tactile and auditory systems first. Visual stimulation that is "out there," beyond the child's reach and tactile involvement, is not enough. *Within this context we can come to understand that vision stimulation techniques off the body of the partially sighted child, such as looking at a flashlight or other light source, are at best entertainment but are not facilitating skill development for active movement and traveling in the world.*

Visual Inefficiency of the Partially Sighted Child and the Solutions for It

The fundamental question is this: how can the partially sighted child be safe, confident, and effective in travel?

The variables below will affect visual functioning in all children and play havoc with partially sighted children. Without the necessary skills of blindness, partially sighted children will be vulnerable during movement and travel.

Use of optics and visual training is not enough to ensure the safety, confidence, and effectiveness of the partially sighted child. Below are some of the variables that compromise the visual efficiency of partially sighted children.

- Light sensitivity and the adjustment to lighting conditions indoors and outdoors.
- Vision reduced at night.
- Reduction in field of view: central, peripheral, blur and blind spots, scars, double vision, and hemianopsia (half-field of vision vertical or horizontal).
- Misperceptions of motion, depth, form and shapes.
- Reduced distance vision and/or near vision.
- Reduced consistency and reliability of efficiency in vision in perceiving size, speed, and color of an object.

Distortions and misleading images resulting in reduced vision and partial sight undermine the child's safety and confidence in travel. *Above all, this should be remembered: O&M is a confidence-based skill. Vision and the effects of the environment are mediated with the alternative skills of blindness.*

The answer to the question of how the partially sighted child can become safe, confident and effective in travel is this: develop proficiency in the use of the cane for independent movement and travel. This is learned best by using sleep shades. Partially sighted children can not rely on their vision alone. No amount of visual enhancement, optical devices or training in using them can provide children with what is required for responsible, safe, confident, effective independent travel. What is needed is a full set of skills available through the learning of alternative non-visual skills. The best tool in learning and implementing the alternative skills of blindness for travel is the cane. This means learning to use the cane and travel with it, thoroughly and confidently by using sleep shades. Of course, partially sighted children should have an understanding of the reason for using sleep shades.

Understanding the needs and vulnerability of partially sighted children and how to reduce their vulnerability with the learning of alternative skills, promotes our understanding of O&M and the role of the O&M specialist in providing a complete package of skills for succeeding with partial sight.

Pushing Partial Sight Vision to the Point of Inefficiency

Partially sighted children are the majority of children being serviced by professional service providers. They are among the legally blind population. Educationally, the conventional approach to utilizing vision in partially sighted children has advanced a vision first agenda, often pushing the vision of these children to the point of inefficiency. *At the expense of not learning non-visual skills, these partially sighted children have been only taught partially learned skills.* Succeeding with partial sight without the skills of blindness will be a precarious journey for these children and often ends in not living up to their full potential.

For example, as the result of placing an importance on developing vision only, partially sighted children have learned to read slower with large print, closed circuit televisions, and low vision devices than their true potential would allow. By learning Braille, slate and stylus, and other nonvisual skills and use of nonvisual materials, partially sighted children are better able to compete on terms of equality with their typically sighted peers.

The consumer movement in blindness through the efforts of the National Federation of the Blind has advanced this understanding of the need for Braille for *all legally blind children (totally blind or partially sighted).* Not to long ago the possibility of Braille being taught to totally blind children was being questioned by professionals. This thinking was partially the result in the overuse of talking books and other speech technology that made print available in auditory form. Fortunately, this is changing due to these efforts of the organized blind, holding professional service providers responsible for teaching Braille to all blind children. Likewise, consumer efforts in advancing the use of the cane and other nonvisual skills in O&M for partially sighted children have planted seeds of change as well. Consequently, the vision first agenda is declining in practice. *The end result of the vision first agenda is this: it has given the partially sighted child and their parents a "raw deal and not the real deal" on how to succeed as full participants in society.*

Nonvisual Skills: The Solution for Success for Partially Sighted Children

Research has shown that blind adults who have the skills of blindness in Braille and cane travel have a higher rate of employment. Literacy skills and travel skills are advanced and learned in the Promotion Model approach. Succeeding with partial sight in O&M involves the following:

- *What matters for success is dependent on the number of skills a child has with which to compete and not the "numbers" describing visual acuity.* It is true that success is in the numbers but the numbers are in the quantity of nonvisual skills, not the quantity of vision. So, start the learning of nonvisual skills early, at the age/stage appropriate time, when the partial sight is not efficient to do the task visually.

- *There must be respect for the partially sighted child as a blind person.* If the partially sighted child is not described as blind but as visually impaired, identifying nonvisual skills that are needed for independence are often overlooked. Most textbooks take great care in advancing the terminology of visually impaired for the description of the (legally blind) partially sighted child. This approach avoids the use of the word blind. By avoiding the word blind to describe a population of children who can benefit from the skills of blindness, how does the parent and the school community develop awareness of the full compliment of needs and skills for the partially sighted child?

    What is this resistance by many professional service providers to describe the child in a way that would produce the greatest benefits? In addition, to describe the legally blind child as partially sighted is an honest and positive description of the visual characteristics of the child, rather than to place the emphasis on "impaired" when describing the child.

- *Respect for the alternative skills of blindness is essential.* The fact is this: blind children at best (20/200 vision) have only 10% of typical vision. How can we expect children to compete on terms of equality when only their weakest sense is being promoted educationally?

    As long as professionals continue to hold onto the outdated theory that 85% of all learning is visual, then the understanding of the value and importance of learning nonvisual skills for partially sighted children will continue to be delayed. Progressive educators today in teaching typically sighted children do not believe in this theory, knowing that sighted children learn in many ways, having multiple abilities to learn. For example some sighted children are more tactile or auditory learners. I have given examples of misguided approaches of "vision stimulation," "functional vision assessments" and the "vision first agenda."

- *Use of sleep shades (blindfold) is a necessary requirement to learn the skills of blindness.* Perhaps the most controversial way to learn the skills of blindness is when sleep shades are used in teaching the alternative skills. The conventional approach does not promote full occlusion but rather partial occlusion (if at all) in the teaching of O&M concepts and skills. The main argument against using sleep shades appears to be this: what is to prevent blind children trained in using sleep shades (full occlusion) to go back to using their limited vision after training?

  The answer to this question is simply that by learning the nonvisual skills thoroughly and efficiently, the children will not go back to use their limited vision in the same inefficient manner. *They will use their vision for what they can see and the cane and other nonvisual skills for what they cannot see. Partially sighted children or ones with such little residual vision will come to develop a confidence base with the nonvisual skills because they were learned without the use of vision.* Partially sighted children will truly believe in themselves, in who they are and what they can accomplish as independent travelers.

- *Use of the cane for partially sighted (legally blind) children puts them at an advantage over using just 10% of typical vision without other nonvisual skills.* The cane is often delayed or not recommended at all for the young blind or partially sighted child. In the early years the vision first agenda advances the use of vision. One result of this thinking is that the cane will cause the child to depend on this tool and not rely on what vision is available to the child. This hits at the core of the misguided approach of the vision first agenda. What could possibly be wrong with the partially sighted child becoming "dependent" on a cane? Are not the "normally" sighted children *dependent* on their vision? By following the logic of this assumption the end result is this: partially sighted children will depend upon visual inefficiency, be stressed out and less safe, but the "good news" is that they will have *depended* on their reduced vision, the less efficient sense.

Some of the many advantages of the cane for the partially sighted traveler include the following: the cane is a low vision travel aid for the partially sighted child (and a no-vision travel aid for the totally blind child); the cane "looks" down so the child can look up and possibly use vision more effectively; the cane increases the field of view by contacting objects to the side that the child may not perceive or visually regard; when touching the ground, the cane gives depth perception information that may be more accurate than partial sight; the use of the cane reduces stress by taking the guess work out of what is ahead and giving the blind child more exact preview than reduced vision provides; and as the cane is tapped side to side, it says to those crossing the path of the partially sighted child, "this is the amount of space I need to be a responsible traveler." How often do partially sighted children bump or fall over objects and people because their vision is not efficient? Sometimes the choice comes down to this: a partially sighted child can look "silly" trying to pass for a typically sighted peer or the child can look blind, confident and capable by using a cane.

- *Nonvisual skills lead to efficient use of vision.* A menu of active movement experiences using nonvisual skills will do more to develop the capacity of the child's partial sight than working on vision alone. The child will learn to use vision in the way that it is naturally useful. Things to see may be things to touch or things to search out, and things to touch may be things to see. Let blind children decide what is the natural use of their own vision.

As a result of not promoting cane travel with partially sighted children, many will use their own feet as two built in canes to detect curbs, steps, and other drop-offs. They will place their feet on the edge, not unlike cane travelers locating the edge of a step with their cane. What do you think is the more efficient method—when partially sighted children use their feet to detect a drop-off at a curb or when they use the cane? By not using a cane, children are more cautious, tentative, stressed out, and exhibit poorer postures as a result of visual misperceptions of what is "down there" or ahead of them in travel.

- *Nonvisual skills put partially sighted children at an advantage.* Blind children who are using age/stage appropriate skills are more likely to be confident in their travel and in communicating their needs to others. For example, partially sighted children are at no greater advantage than totally blind children for having vision if both children are looking for a friend on a playground they cannot see. Children who know to ask the right question and communicate it will get their needs met more quickly. Children must learn to ask, "Where are my friends?" and "Where are they playing—at the slides or the swings?" Children who know what sense to use for what task will be at an advantage.

Partially sighted children will often not speak up because of being vulnerable to others around them thinking they cannot see very well. How many times are partially sighted children asked if they can see something? This sort of investigative type question does not build self-esteem in the partially sighted child.

This chapter has taken a look at educational approaches and practices primarily in early intervention and pre-school. It has reviewed the critical issues regarding inde-pendent movement and travel for the typical developing blind child and the blind child with multiple disabilities. As adults our goal is early intervention to facilitate the independent movement and travel of blind children.

A head-on approach has been used when discussing the contrast between conventional O&M and the Promotion Model. I believe this is needed because the conventional approach is the prevalent O&M program for blind chil-dren. Many of its practices need to be questioned and alternatives given for the independent movement and travel of blind children.

As parents and professional service providers and other adults in the life of blind children, we have a choice to intervene on their behalf or interfere with their develop-ment. The positive, logical, and realistic choice is to pro-mote activities that will develop independent movement and travel. The blind child is capable, willing, and ready to learn. The problem to be fixed is not blindness.

In the words of Eric Hoffer, "fair play is primarily not blaming others for anything wrong with us." We must not blame the children or blame blindness but rather look at whether we are offering a "fair play" to blind children developing to their full capacities in their independent movement and travel.

CHAPTER 4

CANE TRAVEL FOR THE BLIND CHILD—FROM THE BOTTOM-UP

A toddler using a cane is walking away from his stroller

Independent Movement and Travel in Blind Children: A Promotion Model, pp. 143–192
Copyright © 2007 by Information Age Publishing

The first skill of the Inner Game is called "letting it happen."
This means gradually building a trust
in the innate ability of your body to learn and to perform.
—W. Timothy Gallwey

This chapter discusses cane travel for blind children by presenting a "bottom-up" conceptualization of teaching and learning cane travel that is based on the building blocks of the Promotion Model. Central to the independent movement and travel of blind children is the teamwork in which adults must partake to facilitate such independence. I will start with a philosophy for using the cane and proceed to discuss the "teaching cane" approach, the functions of the cane, and the characteristics of the cane. This then sets the stage for understanding when to start using the cane with the blind child and a description of what the beginnings of cane travel usage will look like. The final section of the chapter deals with how to perform the cane skills and discusses the skills the child can be expected to perform at home, school, and community, given adequate and appropriate instruction.

PHILOSOPHY FOR USING THE CANE

No other activity promotes independent movement and travel in blind children *more* than the use of the cane. The value we adults place on the independent movement and travel of blind children has a great deal to do with how they will move in the world. It has been said that *believing is achieving. Therefore, to the extent orientation and mobility (O&M) specialists and parents of blind children believe in the need for independent movement and travel in blind children, the child will achieve to these expectations. Believing in the need leads to achievement!*

What will the movement be like? Will it be dependent or independent, passive, or active? This is not to disregard how developmental delays may impact the blind child's movement. It is to say, however, that the *value* we place on the child's independence in movement and travel *is* the most significant factor in creating a plan and executing that plan to promote the child reaching full potential. We can expect positive outcomes from blind children to be independent travelers if we start with positive values and beliefs about how they will come to know and move in the world.

If valuing the blind child's independent movement and travel is simple to understand, then why do so many parents find it more difficult to achieve for their blind children? It has been my experience that the most formidable obstacle to valuing independent movement and travel in the blind child is negative attitudes. Negative attitudes permeate our society's understanding of blindness. Deficit-thinking about blindness leads to the perception that blindness is not respectable and needs to be fixed. Attitudes of *"blind children need to be helped" overshadow the promotion of learning the age/stage appropriate skills of blindness for independent movement and travel.*

The Promotion Model acknowledges that blind children will take age/stage appropriate responsibility for their own movement and travel needs. *This is a process toward independence and instruction in the use of the cane facilitates this process in a way that no other intervention can. It is a way of thinking and living with blindness that is skill and goal oriented and the goal is independence.* We want to plant the seed that the child will come to develop the self-perception of being an active mover and traveler, deciding where to go and how to get there. We have a responsibility to the child to facilitate and promote this perception.

The most overused method of movement and travel for the blind child is the sighted/human guide. It has been promoted by the majority of professional service providers as the primary way for blind children to move in school and the community during the early years of their development. Additionally, developmentally delayed and multiple disabled blind children are even more vulnerable because many O&M specialists are more *apprehensive* about giving them developmentally appropriate responsibility for their own travel.

Please understand that I am not suggesting that the sighted/human guide is not a respectable method for blind persons to use when moving about. What I am suggesting is this: when the young blind child's concept of moving in the world is developed on the arm of another, this is passive movement, not active movement. From the bottom-up, the child is not learning about how to navigate the world with the cane but walking with someone who is doing the navigation. As the child grows, such extensive guided experiences will limit opportunities for independent movement and travel.

Learning to use the cane is a process that develops over time. It needs to start early in the child's life. *How can the blind child engage in this process in an independent way if we do not place a cane in the child's hand?* And when we do, the most interesting thing happens: adults and sighted peers of the blind children are less likely to "lead" them. With cane in hand, the blind child is sending a message of independence. *As one parent said to me, "the cane answers the questions most people are afraid to ask, and answers it in a positive way."*

THE IMPORTANCE OF THE TEACHING CANE

Because the use of the teaching cane is so central to the bottom-up orientation of the Promotion Model, it will be worthwhile to discuss how the teaching cane evolved, as it is an example of changing professional attitudes and thinking possibilities and not limitations. Its evolution is a testimonial to alternative approaches to conventional O&M to include a new bottom-up perspective.

As a sighted, conventionally trained O&M specialist, the thought of using a cane in instruction to teach blind children never occurred to me for 20 years. I was trained to use my sight to monitor the movements of blind children. Blind children had their canes and I had my sight. The thought occurred to me for the first time when observing blind travel instructors teaching blind students: I began to realize the attunement between the student and the blind instructor. Not only were blind cane travel instructors using their canes for their own travel, but also to give information and role model positive cane travel skills for their students.

It is unfortunate how a mind set of beliefs about the "what" and "how" we do our teaching as professional service providers can cement our mind as well as limit possibilities for different approaches. So, for about a year I did not apply the observation of blind travel instructors to how I could alter my approach with blind children. Then one day, I was going down a hall in an elementary school, walking with my student to her class, as we were going to do a little "show and tell" about the cane. I took out a telescopic cane from my briefcase to show her the cane I would be using for the cane demonstration to her classmates. I tapped it on the floor and walked with her, as she used her cane. This student broke out into a beautiful smile and said, "You use a cane too, Mr. Joe?" I immediately felt shivers up and down my spine, as I could not deny her enthusiasm and interest. I explained that, because I was sighted I use my vision for travel, but for demonstration purposes like we were going to do today with her classmates, I would use a cane.

Then an idea came to me. This student had been having difficulty with sliding and tapping her cane wide enough for adequate coverage. I asked her to listen to my tap and think about the sound my cane made and if she could do the same. Within one minute this kindergarten child expanded her coverage to an adequate width. I never had to place my hand over hers or physically monitor her movement in any way. She simply heard my cane, internalized the information and developed a new motor plan. This is an example of bottom-up learning that this child exhibited and taught me. *From then on I had a new teaching strategy and teaching tool, the "teaching cane."*

Once comfortable using the teaching cane I decided to give parents of blind children the opportunity to learn to use their teaching canes too. Next, I applied the teaching cane concept to classroom teachers and instructional assistants educating blind children. The mystique surrounding cane travel was demystified as I role released my O&M information and teaching cane to the significant others in the blind child's life. This gave the blind child opportunity to practice the cane skills at home and school.

After a few years of using the teaching cane I wondered how it could be used with blind babies. It is not surprising that the answer came from consulting with a family who had a blind baby. One day I was teaching a parent about the cane and how her baby would learn to use it. As this parent held her baby in one arm and held the cane in the other, which came up to her nose, her baby reached out to explore the handle of the cane. As the mother made sliding and tapping motions with the cane, her baby repeated the movements by initiating the movement of the cane. I suggested to the mother that she put her baby on the floor and allow her baby to hold onto shaft of the cane. Once the baby did this, I asked the mother to walk. She did and her baby held on to the cane and walked also, in front of the mother. We were both delighted with the baby's interest and curiosity with the *mother's* teaching cane. As a result of my observing such an activity, I realized I could do this with other parents and I became aware of the advantage of the longer length of the cane when using the teaching cane. If the cane was measured at a conventional O&M length (breastbone/sternum), the baby would not have been able to reach and explore it in the mother's arms. Additionally, when walking, the mother could hold the handle guiding the cane while the baby held onto the shaft. It was long enough to accommodate both "travelers."

The development of the teaching cane was a process of discovery for me, utilizing blind children, their parents, and skilled blind adults. In the Promotion Model the teaching cane is of primary importance for the positive introduction of the cane to the blind baby and preschool blind child. Such an approach can also be used with developmentally delayed blind children who, although older chronologically, are at a younger age developmentally.

FUNCTIONS OF THE CANE

The cane is a hand-held tool used for independent movement and travel. It performs many functions. Under the blind child's direction, it can inform, explore, inspect, detect, protect, and most of all, facilitate getting to know and move in the world.

To illustrate, the cane is more than a "windshield wiper" on the world. It is the "steering wheel" that can be manipulated to where the traveler wants to go and gives direction for whenever the traveler wants to circumvent an obstacle. It is the "headlights" giving preview of what's ahead. It is the "bumper" protecting from unexpected encounters. It is the "antennae" receiving resonance information about the sound space world. It is the "tires," adjusting to the terrain and providing a smoother safer ride. Like the car, the cane is as effective as the "driver," who must obey the "laws of the road." The cane gets children where they want to go.

Below is a list of the basic functions of the cane.

- **Tool Usage:** In the progression of tool usage, the cane is used intelligently by the child to reach off body and touch the world. It is a hand-held tool. With practice, the cane increases the safety, confidence, effectiveness, and efficiency of the child moving about the world.

- **Protector, Detector, and Previewer:** The cane conducts information through its shaft into the blind child's hand. This is often referred to as "feedback." The child, as a traveler, then uses this information to decide how and where to go and what to do to get there. Like vision, the cane tells the child what is ahead, detects what is to be avoided or approached and gives general preview, not only of where the traveler will be stepping next but echolocation information of objects further away.

- **Tool for Action and Sensory Integration:** The cane is a tool for active movement. It gathers information. Sensory integration is what children do with sensory information. The cane facilitates sensory integration, as it is a hand-held tool used by the upper body that "connects" to the ground, and this connection affects the movements of the lower body. Occupational and physical therapists who work with blind children can be given guidance to incorporate the cane into their therapy activities. When this is done therapists find that the use of the cane facilitates sensory integration of information. This occurs because the cane conducts to the child's hand information that travels up the arm into the child's brain.

The cane decreases the need for self-stimulation by increasing the active movement of the blind child in a purposeful and satisfying way. Therapists agree that the less the child needs to think about the movement, the more automatically it will be done. I can think of no other tool that affords such facilitation of this goal of automatic movement with a hand-held tool than with the cane.

- **Tool for Normalizing Posture and Gait:** Use of the long cane assists with the child developing "normal" gait patterns and posture. The research on movement in blind children typically reported a wide-based stance, abnormal gait patterns, poor posture, and constriction of the body when moving. These abnormalities were thought to be due to blindness. We now know otherwise: they were due to lack of opportunity to use the cane. Such a lack in the blind child using the appropriate tool at the appropriate developmental time caused the abnormalities in posture and gait to occur. With the long cane the child can stand relaxed and erect, develop typical gait patterns, and move faster and more confidently.

- **Tool for Play:** Initially, the cane is used and enjoyed by blind children in their play. The child has fun with it, poking it in snow and bushes or exploring a playground. The child taps it on different surfaces for the fun of hearing echoes. In an amusing, fun way the cane introduces the child to the world beyond the fingertips. Use of the cane stimulates the creative and imaginative nature of the child.

- **Low Vision Aid:** The cane can be used by partially sighted children to look where their eyes cannot see, for example, the cane "looks" down or to the side so they can look up. It touches the world for children, offering the possibility that they may want to visually view what it touched. The use of the cane as a low vision aid was covered more extensively in the chapter 3 in the section titled "Succeeding with Partial Sight."

- **Tool for Confidence and Self-Esteem:** O&M *is* a confidence-based skill and the early use of the cane introduces the blind child to experiences that increase self-confidence. When introduced early in life, the cane affirms who the blind child is and what must be done to be independent. The child develops confidence earlier in the "what" and "how" of independent travel. Such confidence integrates into the personality of the child

- **Tool for Freedom of Movement:** The cane affords the opportunities for *freedom of movement and joy of movement that is every child's right.* With it children can decide where and when to go, how fast or how slow. The cane facilitates awareness of the child's own movement and this increases attention span while moving and traveling in the environment.

- **Tool for Cognitive Development:** The cane is a tool that provides opportunities for children to use their intelligence in thinking about self-directed movement, making decisions, developing good judgment and learning to problem solve. Through self-monitoring the child directs the movement of the cane to satisfy curiosity and understand the requirements of safe and effective travel. Driven by cognitive interests, the cane is a tool to learn about the environment. Its use facilitates the formation of basic concepts about the environment and prepares the child for learning more advanced O&M concepts and skills.

- **Puts the Blind Child at an Advantage When Traveling:** The use of the cane has so many functions that it places the child at a real advantage in learning about the world and in moving and traveling in it. Through everyday experiences with the cane, blind children learn through their own orientation and mobility to view themselves as independent travelers. To not get an early start on cane travel for the blind child is to place the child at a disadvantage and all of the aforementioned "functions of the cane" are not a possibility; instead limitations will be developed by the passive movement that following someone's lead engenders. The child's cognitive development, freedom of movement and confidence to travel independently is also at risk of not developing. Make sure the blind child in your care is given all the advantages.

CHARACTERISTICS OF THE CANE

The characteristics of the cane can affect the safety, effectiveness, and efficiency of the traveler. As travelers, blind children and blind adults have the same requirements for the characteristics of the cane. These main characteristics that need to be considered when choosing a cane are: composition, weight, length, grip, tip, flexibility of the shaft, resonance affordability, and one piece or folding.

As blind children mature in developing appropriate posture, balance, hand functioning, height, and size, they will use a proportionately larger cane. Over the years, I have experimented with a variety of types of canes, grips, and tips. I have found that the straight, hollow, flexible, lightweight, metal-tipped canes, such as those available through the National Federation of the Blind, possess the most advantages for the blind traveler. These canes start at about 24 inches and, as their length increases, the overall proportions of the cane are scaled larger. The *design* of the cane is not altered. This creates a seamless continuity for the child and makes it unnecessary to adapt to a different type of cane.

The *characteristics* of the long cane can either afford the traveler advantages in use of this hand-held tool or not. Below is a list with a brief explanation of the characteristics that have the most significant effect on the independent movement and travel of blind children.

- **Composition:** Canes can be made of metal, fiberglass, carbon fiber, and wood. What is important for blind children is that the material used is lightweight and flexible, and is a superior conductor of resonance and tactile information. I have found the materials that facilitate the child's travel most to be fiberglass and carbon fiber.
- **Weight:** Remembering that a cane is a hand-held tool, the lighter cane places children at an advantage over a heavier cane because they can more easily manipulate the use of it by the hand. A cane that is too heavy will compromise hand functioning. The lighter cane approach to travel places children at an advantage.

  With a heavier cane the blind child usually drags it behind or keeps it to the side. This leaves the child vulnerable in front, as the cane is not always clearing ahead. Canes that are too heavy will reduce the control that the child has to manipulate the cane at the wrist, hand and fingers. Easy manipulation of the cane will be reduced. The heavier canes restrict the possibility of a longer cane for younger blind children who need the extra length to compensate for lack of extension of the arm and walking in-step as older blind children and blind adults can do.
- **Length of Cane:** A lightweight cane introduces the possibility for a longer cane to be introduced to the child. The O&M specialist must take into account the fact that the blind child will not extend the arm forward as an adult and not be able to walk in-step.

These are developmentally advanced skills beyond the capability for the young child. Therefore, a child-centered measurement would be around the mouth to nose area. This gives the child more time to react to an object when contacted.

The conventional approach of sternum/breastbone area, as a marker for length, is based on adults of walking in-step, adult reaction time capability, and other adult-based factors. When working with the bottom-up approach, it is understood that the child will not have these same capabilities. Therefore, this rationale for conventional measurement of length of the cane is inadequate.

- **Grip of the Cane:** It is important that blind children be able to place their child-sized hands comfortably around the shaft of the cane. An adult-sized cane that is cut down may be the correct length for the child, but the grip circumference is often too big. Consequently the child cannot grip the cane properly. In addition, some types of child-sized canes on the market have a sponge or rubber type material around the shaft with a section notched out for the pointer finger. In my work with blind babies and cane use, they would often try to bite this material. This, of course, was not safe, as the material is not meant to be chewed and digested.

  A cylinder shaped cane grip makes it easier for the child to "grasp and go" whether the child is right- or left-handed. A grip that has one flat side is obtrusive to the child's natural inclination to hold the cane. In addition, the flat surface is for isolating the index finger, which the younger blind child is not usually ready to do. Also, isolating the index finger is a conventional O&M grip protocol, which is not necessary to hold and use the cane proficiently, as there are alternative grip positions. These are discussed later in this chapter.

- **Tip of the Cane:** The best type of tip for the cane is a *metal* tip cane. The tips of the NFB type canes are metal surrounded by rubber and have a certain amount of flexibility. In this way the blind child can get the crisp, clear information from the metal tip cane and is less likely to get stuck in cracks in the sidewalk, as the child gains experience in handling the various types of terrain. The cane can come with many different types of tips. For example, the marshmallow (rolling and nonrolling), mushroom, and teardrop tips (made of plastic/plastic type materials) were developed because it was *assumed that gliding over uneven surfaces more easily would be a good thing for blind children.*

  My experience has been the opposite, however. By easily gliding or rolling over the ground, these tips reduce the texture information and details of the ground surface. From the bottom-up, blind children need to understand about cracks in the sidewalk, uneven terrain and the more subtle texture differences in ground surfaces. They need to easily identify where the sidewalk, grass and driveway differentiate. A cane tip that subdues this information is not affording *clear* information. In addition, these type tips distort resonance (sound feedback) that the cane *should* afford the child.

- **Flexibility of the Cane Shaft:** It is important for the composition of the cane to have flexibility as it contacts the environment. Fiberglass canes have a certain amount of give and take, can bend and go back to their original shape. Metal canes are easily bent and once bent they do not regain to their original shape. Metal folding canes are the most frequently dispensed canes in O&M instruction even though they easily lose their shape and become deformed at the joint-fit.

In addition, there is the added factor of getting hurt. When moving with the cane, blind children are learning about speed, confronting an object, and reaction time with the cane. Earlier on in learning to use the cane, children can hit an object and continue forward. This results in the cane being pushed into their stomach or groin area. A more flexible cane results in less of a "push" and a more user-friendly understanding of contacting the object world.

- **Resonance and Tactile Feedback Potential of the Cane:** The importance of resonance capability of the cane can not be overstated. The blind child will learn to use resonance for information and orientation, as in echolocation. The importance of tactile feedback is also essential. It gives very useful information about ground surfaces and assists in identifying what type of surface is ahead. Therefore, hollow, one piece canes made of fiberglass are superior conductors of resonance and tactile information. In contrast, folding canes have elastic running down the shaft that distorts and dampens resonance and tactile information, thereby providing much less information to the child.

- **One Piece Hollow Design:** A cane made of a one piece, hollow design construction facilitates vibration and tactile information, as well as resonance for echolocation use, in a superior way that folding canes do not. For the first time traveler it is best to use a one piece, hollow design cane. In addition to facilitating these aforementioned characteristics, such a cane affords the opportunity for the child to learn how to store the cane in the classroom, cafeteria, and the car. When children are given a folding cane, they do not have an opportunity to learn to store a one piece cane.

- **Folding and Telescopic Canes:** *Folding canes should never be used as the blind child's first cane.* Folding canes embody so many *negative* characteristics for blind children. Here are some reasons why:

  1. The elastic running down the shaft of a folding cane dampens and distorts resonance information.
  2. Folding canes add weight and this will reduce the increased length of the cane the child can handle without compromising hand functioning.
  3. Folding canes increase dependence because many young blind in early intervention and preschool children can not fold or unfold their cane; they must rely on someone else to do it for them. This does not facilitate independence.
  4. Folding canes convey negative messages about the cane. What message do we send blind children when we ask them to fold their cane? Is the cane in the way? Should it not be seen? It is the subtle negative messages about the cane that can result in blind children developing poor self-esteem and negative thoughts about the use of the cane.
  5. Telescoping canes have the advantage of having a hollow center and no elastic running down the staff to distort resonance, but they don't offer the stability of the one-piece cane. These canes tend to "telescope in" when they hit an object. Young blind children may not be ready to react quickly enough to this and could bring them in harm's way.

Eventually, a telescoping or folding cane might be an option as a back-up cane, or when the child has developed efficient reaction time and a light touch with using the cane. However, in the early movement of blind children, adults must promote what is known to be best to facilitate independent movement and travel, and which affords a rich and valuable experience in using the cane.

When these characteristics of the cane are considered carefully, we are more likely to choose a cane that places the blind child at an advantage. The bottom line is this: any cane is better than no cane. However, if we are to promote the independent movement and travel of blind children, we should consider the characteristics outlined above. We should be placing blind children at an advantage using what we know has worked successfully when learning to use the cane.

When these characteristics are considered and built into a cane, this becomes the cane of choice for the blind child. There are blind adults who use this cane of choice every day and blind children should have the opportunity to use it too. The Resources chapter gives contact information for purchasing this cane through the National Federation of the Blind.

IDEAS FOR ADAPTING THE CANE FOR THE CHILD

To better meet the needs of the child, it may be necessary to adapt the cane. The cane may need to be adapted for various reasons—hand and finger functioning, keeping the tip oriented down, and differences in the child's developmental level to grip and use the cane. Below are some ways to adapt the cane.

- For some children "building up" a cane grip is needed for better hand functioning. Usually these blind children are working with an occupational therapist. The therapist can assist in finding a grip for the cane that can be more functional. The adaptation might be similar to what is used by the child to hold eating utensils. Consider using a sponge taped down with duct tape and a bicycle grip slipped over the shaft of the cane.

- For the child who has not yet learned to keep the cane down, weight can be added. For example, tape a fish weight at the end of the cane, just above the tip. This will not distort the resonance as much as the large plastic tips discussed previously. For some children who need a heavier downward orientation a 3–6 inch piece of metal plumbing pipe may be added, depending on how high the child is lifting the cane off the ground when walking. Put the cane tip end through the hollow pipe, taking the cane tip off first and then putting the cane tip back on and taping down the pipe.
- Velcro and "therapy putty" can be used to attach the cane to the child's desk vertically if placing it underneath the desk or table is not an option. Velcro can also be used as a marker for where to hold the cane for going up stairs or the "shorten-position" for navigating through crowded areas, as discussed later in this chapter.
- Some children like the feeling of an edge at the end of the cane that they can feel in the palm of their hand. A rubber band twisted around the grip end can provide such an edging or a piece of Velcro taped to the end.
- Some children prefer a different feeling on the grip, perhaps a material that is softer. Taping over a thin sponge can create such a cushioned feeling.

These modifications can be removed as the child develops more advanced hand functioning, control over inadvertently lifting the cane, or when personal preferences for griping the cane change.

WHEN TO START
CANE TRAVEL WITH BLIND CHILDREN

In my years of teaching O&M, my thinking has changed about the readiness of blind children to travel with a cane. *What changed over time was not the blind child, but my perception of the child's abilities and readiness. It is this area of "what we think we know" that shifts over time.* Thirty-five years ago, if I had observed my students more carefully, many more blind children would have had the opportunity to develop independent movement and travel concepts and skills much earlier in life. I did not understand then the importance and possibilities of the cane. I now know that the cane, more than any other tool, facilitates movement and travel in this process toward independence.

Usually, but not always, the cane can be introduced after the blind child begins to walk. Yet, I have known blind children who have taken their *first* steps in open space with the cane. In such cases, the child is ready to walk but is not initiating the "stepping into space" and the cane has been found to facilitate movement in this situation. Therefore, observe the blind child's movement around the event of walking and if the cane seems to promote movement, go with it. Before the event of walking some blind babies and developmentally delayed children, when sitting, may enjoy tapping the cane and sliding it on the floor in front of them to contact objects out of arm's reach. There are many creative uses for the cane from the bottom-up perspective.

For the Blind Child Under Three Years of Age

Contrary to conventional O&M, the Promotion Model advocates introducing the cane earlier, rather than later in a child's life, to facilitate independent movement and travel. The time to start cane travel is when it facilitates the movement of the child. This is usually soon after the child has learned to walk.

For children under 3 years of age it is understandable that O&M specialists conventionally trained are not sure when to begin cane travel. They want to act responsibly but may not know how. Their training did not prepare them for teaching the baby in early intervention. What their training did provide, however, were the *readiness concepts of precane skills and precane devices.*

Over the years the "readiness curriculum" of conventional O&M has been greatly expanded. This can cause a delay in when to begin with the cane. The priority of the sighted/human guide and precane coming before the use of the cane makes the blind child vulnerable to a delay in learning age/stage appropriate independent movement and travel skills. In the Promotion Model, learning the cane is *readiness* for independent travel and is given emphasis over use of the sighted/human guide and precane device.

Precanes

Precanes, the term often used for alternate mobility devices (AMDs), implies that the structure and function of the device fits into some continuum of progression for travel tools, and that once the child has mastered this device, the cane would be the next tool. Within the conventional O&M approach, starting out with a precane, assumes "as fact" that some device must be used prior to a cane or as an alternative to it.

Many of these precanes are made of PVC pipe constructions, like the T-shaped cane with roller tip. The components of movement needed to use many of these devices are actually more complex and/or cumbersome than the simple function and design of the cane. Additionally, how will the child go up and down steps with such precane devices that require two hands for their use? The conventional approach suggests the child should place the device over the shoulder. This would mean that blind children would need to balance the precane for a nonuse purpose in addition to balancing themselves. At least with using the cane to go up and down steps the child will learn to manage the cane and body movements for a purposeful skill. In addition, a blind child's posture and gait is negatively affected with conventional pre-cane approach when going up and down steps.

The Promotion Model asserts that the cane—not a precane—should be given to the child first, as soon as it facilitates independent movement and travel. When the cane is given early in the lives of blind children, they demonstrate age/stage appropriate gait, posture, hand functioning and independent movement and travel skills. This sets the stage for the children learning more advanced cane travel skills and being independent moving and traveling about home and school like their sighted peers.

Additionally, when we give a precane, we send a message to the parent: "your child is not ready for a cane." Are our assumptions so solid and based on fact that the child is not ready for the cane that we should be sending this message? Professionals who advocate the use of precanes do so because they feel that the child, who hasn't mastered "appropriate" conventional adult-centered skills, will be unsafe while moving and exploring with the cane.

Of course the young blind child will be under adult supervision when moving about the world. What child younger than three years of age, in preschool or the elementary grades, isn't monitored? All children are supervised in their early movement. Sending a message to parents that a pre-cane will make their child safer could be misleading. Parents might begin to think the child needs less supervision. Sighted toddlers do not initially scan visually or link cognitive and motor plans efficiently, so they will fall and bump into objects. Blind children will do this too with the cane. Blind and sighted children both need supervision and developmental guidance.

When a child's travel tool promotes the sense of security and autonomy in free movement, as the cane does, then much more brainpower is available for orientation and enjoying the feeling of the movement itself. All too often, however, the cane is perceived as the tool of last resort. *"When will the child be ready?" and "How will the child learn?" are really the central questions.* The answer is when the cane facilitates movement for the child to explore the object world and increases confidence in moving about in it. The best way to know is to observe the child. The child who takes to a travel tool "like a duck to water," as many blind children take to the cane, is telling the adult what is best and when to begin.

For the Blind Child in Preschool

O&M specialists and parents of blind children are more confident about readiness for preschoolers to be using the cane than readiness for babies. In more recent years O&M specialists are more aware of the importance of cane travel for blind preschool children and the older arguments for delaying cane use with preschoolers are being debunked, such as:

- Preschoolers lack the motor control to use the cane.
- Preschoolers might hurt other children with the cane.
- Preschoolers will develop bad habits and the learning of appropriate skills later will be negatively affected.

- Preschoolers are familiar with home and school and do not need a cane.

We know that preschool children can learn to be responsible with a cane and that they have the motor control commensurate with their stage of development and are no more likely to hurt another child than their sighted peers are with the tools they use. Yet the conventional approach still promotes precanes for this population as well. Years ago, Dr. Fredric K. Schroeder gave the best example of why preschool blind children can use a cane. He discussed sighted peers scribbling with crayons and made the observation that this activity did not delay their learning to print the alphabet. Likewise the young blind child learning to use the cane is no more likely to develop bad habits later in life with the early "scribbling" on the ground with the cane.

Another delay for initiating the cane with preschoolers is the vision first agenda, which advances the use of partial or residual vision first and training in the use of the cane second. Although attitudes are changing in a more positive direction for partially sighted children to use canes for independent movement and travel, the perception that partially sighted preschool children can meet all of their travel needs overshadows consideration of using the cane as well. In the Promotion Model, observation is essential, not vision. The cane provides blind children with the preview that they need for independent movement and travel.

The fact that teachers and other school staff may be overmonitoring with verbal or tactile prompts the movement of partially sighted children is usually not noticed because the expectation is that they "need help" and gradually will learn to be visually efficient. Therefore, a different standard is used with partially sighted children than children with typical vision who may need some prompting but certainly not as much as partially sighted children.

Since whether the child is functional or not relies on how we adults *perceive* the child's behavior, there needs to be a standard for teachers to follow. What they often do not realize is that the standard is what the typically sighted child is doing. The solution for totally blind or partially sighted children to achieve as their sighted peers should be based on the alternative, nonvisual skills that are needed, regardless of any amount of vision possessed, to be monitoring their own age/stage appropriate independent movement and travel.

For the Blind Child in Grade School

When considering a cane for an older blind child, the reasons for using one may seem more obvious. For example:

- The child is not relaxed in self-monitored (solo) movement.
- The child's stress level is elevated in congested and/or unfamiliar areas.
- Street crossings or night travel is not age/stage appropriate.
- The child's gait and posture are negatively affected by not using a cane.
- The child can not manage the travel situation safely or confidently without having a hand held by an adult.
- The child is experiencing movement on the arm of another person as the main means of getting around.

For these reasons the use of the cane should be initiated. It would seem incredulous that totally blind children would not be using a cane by the time they are in grade school. This, however, is not as rare as it seems. I have worked with totally blind children who prefer to travel with a sighted/human guide and not to use a cane at all. Some of them were in high school. This, I believe, is the result of a blindness system that promoted the use of the guided technique in the early years to such an extent that these children have such negative attitudes about using a cane and also cannot perceive themselves as independent travelers with the cane.

As discussed in Chapter 3, the use of the cane puts partially sighted children at an advantage. However, many partially sighted children in intermediate and high school have negative attitudes about being perceived as blind. They associate the cane with blindness, and therefore, do not use it for their travel, especially when the attempt is made to introduce the cane for the first time during these school years.

Why are the parents of these children not promoting the use or earlier use of the cane? Are we to believe the parents do not care about the well-being of their child? Or is it that they too have negative attitudes about the blindness and the nonvisual skills and tools that could assist their child? And if so, where did the parents acquire such attitudes?

When looking at the big picture we know the negative attitudes about blindness of society. As O&M professionals we have a responsibility to inform these parents of the need for independent movement and travel in their child. We must provide a corrective affect to society's negative attitudes and promote positive attitudes and thinking about the early start to cane travel. We must provide the appropriate instruction at the appropriate time so that blind children achieve the movement and travel skills as are their sighted peers. O&M is a process toward independence and we have the responsibility, in partnership with the parents and school, to initiate this process early in the child's life.

Description of the Beginnings of Cane Travel—What it Looks Like

The young blind child will initially respond to the cane with curiosity, amusement and a desire to explore possible uses for it. Blind children will relate the use of the cane to their developmental level. The blind child will first use exaggerated movements to explore the cane. Some exploratory uses will look like play. This occurs for several reasons: balance, the newness of the tool, and experimenting with movements that can be done with it, such as sliding and banging it. As the child becomes familiar with the cane, movement with the cane will become more refined, purposeful and efficient. Please know that what appears to be the young child playing with the cane is the natural way of learning to use the cane and "work it out." Play is the work of the child, so don't be discouraged if the child's initial reaction to the cane is to "just" play with it.

Accordingly, do not insist on the blind child demonstrating top-down, adult-type skills, such as proper grip, extension of the arm, arc of cane, and touch technique. Such skills will develop as the child matures and gains experience with the cane. If you expect skills the child is not able to perform, you will only frustrate the child and a negative attitude may develop towards the cane. Keep it light and fun, especially with the child under age three. One definition of a baby is a child under 3 years of age. How many sighted children are ready for instruction under 3 years of age? Gradually, with developmental guidance from the O&M specialist and the parent's reinforcement, the child will be able to perform more standard looking cane skills.

The cane will be used at the level of the child's motor development. Children will be able to control the use of the cane with the hand skills they have at the developmental level they are using the cane. For example, initially the child may hold the cane like a shepherd's staff (with the thumb on top), using it for balance as the child walks around. Then the child will hold it more like a golf putter (with the thumb pointing down). With maturation the components of movements, particularly in the wrist, hand, and fingers become more refined.

When blind children touch an object with the cane, they will want to check what is being contacted. You might notice the child's hand sliding down the shaft of the cane to "see" what is being contacted. Sometimes you might observe the child's foot sliding to check the object out also. The child is just trying to get "connected" to the cane and understand how it connects to the object world. Remember, development progresses on body before off body. The cane is a tool that is used off body, reaching out into space. It initially must be integrated with the child's own body. So it's natural for the child to use the foot to verify what the cane is doing. It's really smart on the child's part and a basic bottom-up behavior. Blind children enjoy exhausting all the possibilities of what the cane can do.

Just as vision directs sighted children to where they want to go, where the "action is," the cane puts the blind children where the action is also. All children are learning in the early years to label and identify their world. Blind children are no different. They need to label their world too. *You can not identify and label the world for the child by touching it for the child. The experience is in the self-initiated action.* Touch and movement with the cane facilitate action, contributing to the creation of an active learner.

Once the blind child has responded to the guidance of the professional service provider and parent and is familiar enough with the cane, orienting it to the ground, placing it out in front for information, then the child is ready for more specific suggestions on how to use it. When thinking about the following behaviors, keep this in mind: when they are ready, children will perform the skill being offered by the professional service provider and the parent.

Here are some suggestions on how to proceed and to explain to children what the new information from the cane is telling them. You are the translator of what the information is about and you are modeling for children the proper technique with your teaching cane.

- Children like to slide the cane, so suggesting a "constant contact" is not difficult. This means sliding the cane side to side on the ground. The width of the sweep should be a little wider than the child's width to offer adequate coverage (protection). Practice with sliding the cane to touch each side of a door opening or sliding the cane between two chairs placed a little wider than the child's body can give the idea of how wide to slide. Also, listening to the adult's teaching cane slide side-to-side is very useful.

- By sliding the cane the child will be able to detect drop-offs, such as steps and curbs, more easily. Initially, the feeling of the cane dropping off a step will not be detected by the very young child. This will come with comprehension of what is going on in the movement downward of the cane and with many experiences of feeling the cane go downward.

- When the cane is being used to "look" at a wall to either "see" where it leads or get to a destination, the cane can be held in the hand farthest from the wall. This positions it diagonally across the body for protection. The child can use the hand closest to the wall to look at the wall if so desired. In this way the child is using both sides of the body to acquire information about the environment, learn about how far the wall is and what objects are along the wall. This is part of discovery and exploring. This is not "trailing" as used in the conventional adult-centered approach, which is used to get from one place to another by following the straight-line direction that the wall may provide. Instead, it is about learning from the bottom-up about the objects that fill up space.

- Children need to learn to use the cane with both hands. Children will have a dominant hand, as most children will, but they should be comfortable with using the cane in both hands. There will be times when the cane must be switched for travel requirements, for example, going up and down stairs. We don't want a blind child to get fixed into one way of using the cane. Gradually, as the child gains control of the movement of the cane, other cane skills can be introduced.

DEVELOPMENTAL CONSIDERATIONS FOR BASIC CANE SKILLS

This book places a spotlight on considerations for early learning of O&M, independent movement and travel, using a bottom-up, child-centered approach that offers an alternative to the top-down, adult-centered conventional O&M approach. It also addresses the continuum of learning independent movement and travel skills for the blind child.

Use of the cane by the blind child is a nonvisual skill alternative to use of vision for the sighted child for movement and travel independence. The bottom-up approach works best when the blind child is using a cane. Independent movement and travel skills are more likely to carry over into adulthood when the child gets an early start with the cane. Just as the sighted child gets an early start by using sight to develop age/stage appropriate skills in independent movement and travel, so too the blind child must be given the same opportunity with the cane. For a more in depth understanding of the continuum of cane travel skills used by blind persons of all ages, the Resources chapter provides a list of several valuable books.

Below is a basic outline of independent movement and travel skills used by children as cane travelers within the context of the Promotion Model.

INDEPENDENT MOVEMENT AND TRAVEL SKILLS WITH THE CANE

First Movement Experiences with the Cane

- **Using the Teaching Cane:** The first introduction to the cane may be with the use of the parent's teaching cane. First, while holding the child in one arm and the cane in the other, the child can explore touch interactions with the cane, eventually moving it with the parent and then initiating movements. When the child is able to walk, the child can hold onto the shaft of the parent's teaching cane. While holding onto the shaft of the parent's teaching cane, the child will be in front of the parent. In this way the parent can guide the movement of the cane by standing behind the child. The child will also initiate movements with the teaching cane. Together, the parent and child will explore possibilities with the teaching cane.
- **Hold Cane for Cane Walking:** The cane is held in travel grip position that is developmentally appropriate for the child. The child may hold the cane like

a shepherd's staff or a golf putter, which means with the thumb on top or pointed down, respectively. The child may want to hold the cane halfway down the shaft for better balance and control or at the very end of the grip, feeling the end of the cane in the palm of the hand. Often the very young blind child wants to hold the cane with two hands. Interestingly, this brings the cane to midline (stomach) area. This bottom-up, two-handed approach created by the child offers an alternate approach to beginning cane travel that I often suggest to children who are holding the cane to one side and are not "covering" fully to protect the front of their body.

There are many variations for holding the cane and there are many reasons for it. Sometimes the reason is easy to understand and sometimes it is a mystery. What is important to remember is that the child is doing it for a *reason* and it is best to respect the child's decision, as long as it is safe for the child.

- **Walking with Someone:** Initially, the baby, toddler or child will hold onto the parent with one hand and the cane with the other. *Introduction of the cane should not mean "loss" of the parent or adult's hand but rather an addition to what is familiar to the child—the adult's hand.* This consideration is of particular importance to the developmentally delayed blind child who may have experienced walking with the parent for a much longer period of time than the typical blind child.

Gradually, with the stability that comes with balance and confidence in movement, the child then moves away from the parent contact and ventures out more independently. When cane travel is delayed in blind children, they become accustomed to holding on to the parent's hand, usually for a longer period of time than is age/stage appropriate.

As children gain experience with the cane, they will hold the cane directly out in front of the body. At this time children will begin to explore sliding and tapping the cane. Children may be holding onto the parent's teaching cane, their own cane or both, in making such experimenting movements with the cane. With the cane in hand, the child will be along-side the parent first and then, over time, move in front of the parent.

- **Standing Position:** When children are standing still, teach them to hold the cane upright. Children need to understand and learn that the cane can get in someone else's way when unnecessarily put out in front when standing alone or standing and talking to someone. It is best placed in a vertical, upright posi-tion. While standing still and holding the cane, the child may inadvertently, unexpectedly or purpose-fully slide the cane out in front or exhibit some other "play" behavior and can surprise passers by and this may cause the person to trip over the cane. We want to limit the perception of the cane as a dangerous tool. This begins with teaching the child proper han-dling of the cane.

- **Cane Down on the Ground:** The cane is a travel tool that must be oriented down to contact and survey the ground. Blind babies enjoy banging the cane and lifting the cane high in the air to explore as they get connected to the cane and to the object world. This is understandable. The blind child will gradually lower the cane to the ground. At first the child does not understand that a simple movement in the wrist can elevate the cane so high. Have the child observe your wrist and hand movement with your teaching cane. Playing games with the child to locate objects above and on the ground can give experience with the "wrist feeling" of orienting the cane down. The top-down approach of simply saying, "keep the cane on the ground" will not register with the young traveler as quickly as older children or when adults are beginning to learn how to use the cane.

Remember, for the child "out of the experience comes the concept." The concept is not already in the child's head at such a young age. Sometimes we can add a bit of weight to the cane to assist the child who is having difficulty understanding or perceiving the wrist movement. This is usually the baby or the child who is functioning on the level under 3 years of age. The goal is to orient the cane down to the ground while not compromising hand functioning. The child must be able to easily move the cane.

- **Side to Side and Slide it Wide:** In this technique, also known as "constant contact," the cane is in contact with the ground or floor. This creates a more thorough coverage of the terrain ahead of the child so that uneven surfaces and drop-offs are less likely to surprise the young traveler. The blind child likes the rhyming of this phrase "side-to-side and slide it wide" and this facilitates sustaining the task of sliding the cane.

  Make up games to provide practice with this skill. For example, place milk cartons or plastic bowling pins at random on the floor and let the child knock them all down. If the child is working with physical or occupational therapists, they will have many creative suggestions on how to play with the cane in their respective therapies. The very young blind child will not be able to learn in-step rhythm with the cane until an older age. Therefore, the sliding technique is an important skill that will be used prior to learning the more efficient and advanced cane skills.

How to Use the Cane for Travel

- **Crowded Areas, Walking in Line, the Shorten-Up Position, and the Pencil Grip:** Gripping the cane further down the shaft to reduce the length of the cane's reach can make it more manageable for children. Older children can hold the cane like a pencil. This requires a higher level of hand functioning. Both of these skills enable the blind child to move in more congested areas or in a line with more ease. Because line walking is a very important part of the school day, we want the child to be successful at this task independently. With the "shorten-up" position the blind child's cane will not extend passed or through the legs of other children as easily when line walking or in a crowded area. The child will be able to control the movement of the cane to locate the heel of the person in front and stop or slow down. Sliding the cane with the "shorten-up" technique is a very efficient way for the young cane traveler to walk in line or in crowded areas.

  As children mature in hand functioning development, they will learn to hold the cane in the "pencil grip" position. This grip comes from the organized blind and offers a superior way compared to the conventional approach to manage crowded areas or line walking. Holding the cane *like a pencil*, the child moves the cane closer in or further away from the body as needed. There are as many variations to the pencil grip position as there are for holding an actual pencil. Be careful not to insist on one particular position. What we are aiming at here is functionality, not a single, proper approach.

- **Cane the Wall:** Children use the cane to touch the wall for information or to find a line of direction. The conventional approach may refer to this as "trailing a wall." In the context of the bottom-up approach, this is not about this adult-centered skill per se. It is about a blind child using the cane to "get to know the wall" and the objects that might be alongside it. After the child learns about "wallness" and the many objects, openings, corners, alcoves and intersections that might be encountered, the cane will be used less for exploring and more for using the wall to locate a destination.

The difference from the trailing concept is that the child will not *follow* the wall for a long period of time. In the conventional approach trailing a wall was a technique to enable the adult blind to get from one place to another or to avoid walking in open space with or without a cane. We do not want blind children to avoid walking in open space. But we *do* want the child to learn bottom-up about the characteristics of a wall.

- **Scan:** This skill is the using of the hand(s) or the cane to observe, "look" at objects, as on a long counter or along a wall. The word "scan" is a more *neutral* term than trailing. When blind children are checking out the world they are not lagging behind, which is one definition of trail. Instead, the child is just "looking" for what is available.

- **Middle of Hallway Walking:** As children learn more about walls, corners, and where the wall leads, they will naturally move to the middle of the hall for safer, more convenient and more efficient travel. Walking in the middle of the hallway is safer for children, as their bodies are not near the doors that open up unexpectedly from the classrooms. Also, by walking in the middle of the hallway children are not slowed down by the many objects that might be along the wall that the cane will contact and need to circumvent. Usually, the blind child's echolocation gives information about where the wall is located. This information can be used to understand "middle of hallwayness."

- **Switch Hands:** The child should learn to use the cane in either hand. Blind children will need to learn to hold and learn to use the cane in either hand so they will have the flexibility to do a variety of tasks, such as going up and down stairs or scanning a wall. If the child learns flexibility instead of a rigid way of holding the cane from the beginning, it will be easier to use the cane in either hand later on. Start from the beginning using either hand. What the child is introduced to first will be the way the child will want to do it. This is often true of adults as well. The way we human beings learn something for the first time is the way we seem to want to continue it. In addition, the blind child may not always use the cane with the dominant hand.

- **Stair Technique:** When going up stairs, think "thumb up"! When going down stairs, hold the cane in the shepherd's staff position or pencil grip. If length of the cane seems to get in the way of the blind child going up and down stairs, try these approaches. Have the child hold the cane lower down the shaft when going up the stairs. This ensures that the child will not trip over the cane. Blind children have differing abilities to extend the arm forward holding the cane when going up stairs. Therefore, holding the cane lower down the shaft compensates for the child not being able to extend the arm. A marker for where to hold the cane when going up steps can be useful. A piece of tape or Velcro will do the trick.

  If the child holds the cane for cane walking when going down steps, the cane will reach down to the next step and the child and the cane will not be on the same step at the same time. With practice, the child will learn to understand this information through the cane. As the child becomes more developmentally able to fully extend the arm with the cane, it can then be held at full length going down stairs. The child will be better able to understand the feedback from the cane and know the exact location of the tip of the cane with practice.

- **Drop-Off:** Drop-off occurs when the cane moves from a level surface to a lower point, such as stairs and curbs. The drop-off clue alerts the child to when there is a downward movement of the cane. The cane is a tool for depth perception. The tactile system receives the drop-off information. Vision is not the only way to detect depth, as the tactile system is also accurate when using a cane. For partially sighted children relying on their compromised vision to detect depth, the tactile system is superior.

  It will take time for the blind child to develop proficiency at detecting and responding to this change in depth. This is one reason why a longer cane is useful because the child gets preview of the drop-off further away from the body and has more time to react. Initially, the child will move slowly to the drop-off point, thereby bringing the cane closer to the body and positioning the body at the edge of the step or curb. In time the child will move more fluidly and handle a drop-off with ease and greater speed.

- **Clearing Technique:** When stepping up or down a curb or the last stair on steps, the child should slide the cane side to side to detect any objects that may be in the path of travel. In my own personal training, while learning to use the cane under sleep shades, this was the one skill that took me awhile to remember to employ. I would forget to "clear" and consequently I bumped into objects. Finally, tired of the contacting objects unexpectedly and unnecessarily, I learned this skill. Most blind children will learn in this way too. This is also the skill used in stepping down off a curb to cross a street and, once crossed, used again before stepping up onto the sidewalk.

- **Gathering Information:** Blind children use a variety of informational clues to travel as sighted children do. Children need landmarks for orientation and information from the different sensory systems in order to move effectively around the world. *We want to send the message to the blind child that what is needed is information and not vision.* Children need to learn to ask for information and extract clues from the environment. They need to understand that this is *their responsibility.*

  All too often, adults are obtrusively available to the blind child. For example, adults tell blind children the information they need to know without first asking them questions that are age/stage appropriate. Blind children need to learn this *process* of information gathering. Adults should start in the early development of the blind children with more information, and as the children mature, offer less information; instead, ask questions to help facilitate children figuring it out for themselves.

- **Echolocation:** Echolocation is a sound localization skill—using reflected sound to locate the presence of objects, openings, and closures in the environment. Using the sound space world is natural to a blind child. It functions as an auditory "figure-ground." Using a cane rich in resonance facilitates echolocation.

  Echolocation is a more subtle use of the sound space world to navigate more effectively and safely while using a cane. When a cane is chosen that affords a high level of resonance feedback, then the child is more likely to use echolocation with the cane and the effectiveness and efficiency in movement and travel is facilitated. Children can be taught to voluntarily use echolocation in their movement and travel. It becomes one of the ways to gather information about the environment to facilitate orientation.

- **Long/Short Hallway Sound:** Echolocation is a skill that utilizes the sounds made by the cane being tapped to determine the characteristics of a space, destination to be traveled and distance from that destination. In a hallway a blind child can tap the cane and extract information about the length of the hallway. For example, the blind child may come out of the classroom but not remember whether to turn right or left to go to the bathroom at the end of the hall, far from the door of the classroom. Or the child may be developmentally not ready to consistently use left and right. By tapping the cane the child can get the "long hallway sound" and this information is used to direct movement. The child can also use the cane to get a "short hallway" sound as well. Many blind children are able to use this skill before developing directionality (knowing where left or right is located).

More Advanced Indoor and Outdoor Cane Travel Skills

- **Shorelining:** Shorelining is a conventional O&M term that means using the two edges that lie together along the ground to get a line of direction or to gain information for travel, for example, the edge created by grass along a concrete sidewalk. By shorelining, the child can locate the intersection of sidewalks. Walking along the beach a child could locate the water line and, literally, the shoreline.

Rolling tip canes, usually shaped like a marshmallow, roll over information that could be useful to the child and can interrupt the learning and using of shorelining. It is much more difficult to differentiate a blacktop driveway surface from a cement sidewalk surface with a roller tip cane than with a metal tip cane.

- **Two-Point Touch Technique:** After the child learns to keep the cane down on the ground and slide for information, then gradually the cane can be tapped left and right, one step, one tap, creating a low arc that is about an inch or two off the ground. This is known as "two-point touch" or "touch technique." The two-point touch technique of the cane traveler is a very useful skill. It enables the traveler to move more quickly. A lighter cane with a metal tip can easily be tapped side to side by the child.

Walking on grass introduces the blind child to lifting the cane off the ground. This facilitates the learning of the two-point touch technique because the cane can not be easily slid as it was on the school floor or many sidewalks. On the other hand, when using a marshmallow type tip, this will not happen. The tip glides over the grass and other uneven surfaces, and does not permit the same opportunity to lift the cane up off the ground. Canes with these tips are easier to be pushed forward by the blind child than to tap side to side. These cane tips slow the speed with which the child can walk.

Learning the touch technique is important and necessary as it sets the stage for the learning of in-step rhythm, a skill that maximizes safety and efficiency during travel. When choosing a cane for a blind child, consider the characteristics of the cane that facilitate an efficient two-point touch technique.

- **In-Step Rhythm:** Eventually the child will tap the cane to the opposite side of where the foot is stepping. The cane is tapped to the right as the child is stepping to the left and vice versa. This is one of the more advanced skills taught in cane travel. The instructor or parent must understand that this in-step rhythm is beyond the developmental level of most children under first grade.

I have taught blind children who were able to learn the idea and perform rudimentary in-step rhythm movements with the cane as young as 4 years of age, but it was at a great expense to their safety and efficiency in travel. These children could not perform these motor acts and *also* attend to the other information and skill requirements of using the cane. For the most part, not until first grade can the typical blind child start learning in-step use of the cane. Additionally, there are children (and adults) who can't or prefer not to use the cane with the in-step rhythm. Once again, this is why the longer cane approach to travel puts the traveler at an advantage. The extra length of the cane still protects the child not walking in-step. The marshmallow tip canes encourage the pushing and sliding and do not encourage in-step rhythm. The added weight of these canes limits the extra length needed by the child to compensate for not walking in-step.

Whether it is by choice or by necessity, there will be times when walking in-step is not possible, circumventing around an obstacle, for example. The longer cane approach to travel solves the problem. It is sound philosophically, from a developmental point of view and from the adult point of view.

- **Sidewalk Walking:** Blind children will learn about "sidewalkness," "curbsideness," and "building-side-ness" through exploration with their cane and practice, practice, practice. Eventually they will be able to walk down the middle of a sidewalk.

  The same process that worked for learning "hall-way walking" indoors can be used for sidewalk walking as well. This is starting from the boundaries, the curb and building and working in, a very bottom-up approach. In addition, while learning to walk on a sidewalk the child will learn, as all children do, to pay attention to driveways. Also, the blind child can learn how to use echolocation to locate an alley, recessed entrance to a store or the end of a building. By showing the blind child the environmental layout of the objects that define spaces when walking on a sidewalk, we will facilitate concepts of orientation and the travel skills that will put the child at an advantage for learning more advanced travel concepts and skills later in life.

- **Concept of a Block:** Walking on a sidewalk naturally progresses into learning about "what's around the corner of the block." Blocks usually have four sides. It is fun for children to learn that they can go around four sides and end up where they started. The block provides a finite boundary that can teach many orientation skills, such as memory, sequencing of information and extracting clues from the environment.

  Walking around a block promotes security in dealing with the big world out there, because the child can not get lost in this controlled space. Each side of the block can be thought of as one side to a classroom with its distinguishing aspects that make it stand out in the child's mind.

By using the cane, the child can gather tactile and auditory information about each side of the block with its distinguishing characteristics. This develops tactile and auditory memory skills that are so important for independent movement and travel. Walking around a block is fun and offers many possibilities for learning about independent travel.

- **Traffic, Intersections, and Street Crossings:** It is important to learn about the movement of cars on the street, the parallel and perpendicular traffic patterns that they form, what controls the traffic at intersections, and how to cross a street with the cane. When learning to walk on a sidewalk the child will gradually become more aware of the sounds of cars, buses, trucks, and other vehicles on the roadway. In time the O&M specialists introduces the idea of traffic alongside (parallel) and traffic in front (perpendicular). Early learning of the various types of intersections, two-way stop, a four-way stop, and a "T" intersection, the child is introduced to the variety of traffic patterns that can exist.

  Blind children will have a more complete understanding of concepts when the information and experiences that have been provided to them are varied and complete. Blind children need to have full disclosure of what is available in the environment. They need to understand what controls the traffic at intersections, such as a stop sign, one way street, traffic light, or traffic guard. It sets the stage for learning more advanced O&M concepts and skills that apply to these various traffic patterns.

  Learning to cross a street with a cane necessitates orientation concepts and cane travel skills. The two-point touch technique and/or in-step rhythm will be relied on for quick and efficient movement across the street. The child will learn to use the drop-off clue to locate the curb and clearing technique when stepping up from the street onto the sidewalk. The child will learn to listen to parallel and perpendicular traffic and pick the correct moment to cross.

Therefore, there are a number of skills that come together when learning to cross a street. Learning these skills gives the child confidence in mastering a very important life skill that all children need to learn. Sighted children are expected to learn to cross streets with age/stage appropriate independence and so the same expectations are needed for blind children. Just as sighted children will learn to visually scan and listen for traffic to cross streets independently, so too blind children will learn to scan with the cane and use auditory information. When given adequate and appropriate instruction, the blind child can learn this independent life skill as well.

- **Cardinal Directions:** Learning about north, south, east, and west, using a Braille compass, sun location, and street references are all part of learning about what direction the traveler is headed. Learning about cardinal directions is a process that starts with the child's own understanding of front, back, side, making an about face, and a 90-degree turn. The understanding of spatial concepts is a developmental process best accomplished through the child's own active movement. The blind child's active movement is best done with the cane.

  On the other hand, if blind children learn to move more passively about the environment, for example, if they are guided, they will not learn about how to navigate in space. While on the arm of another person there will be a delay in children's understanding of cardinal directions in reference to their own body.

Using the cane while understanding cardinal directions empowers blind children to move and explore more on their own and experience the freedom and personal enjoyment that independent movement and travel can offer.

- **Exploring The Environment:** Place a high value on children exploring the environment and discovering for themselves information about the object world. In the early years of play and movement blind children will learn about their relationship to objects and the spatial relationship of those objects to other persons, places and things. This learning can only occur if children are given free time to explore and discover. As mentioned earlier, much time at home, early intervention, preschool and elementary school, is spent by the blind child in structured time when blind children are expected to perform the tasks given them. Free time must be built in as well. From early intervention to grade school, blind children must have free time to explore and discover. They can do this best with the cane.

- **Sleep Shades:** Sleep shades are blindfolds used to cover the eyes of cane travelers when learning nonvisual skills of blindness. When working with the young blind child, it is important to inform the parent and school staff of the intent and use of sleep shades.

  When the idea is introduced in a positive light, the use of sleep shades is met with full cooperation. Often the child considers sleep shades fun. They can be introduced to the whole class of preschool children, for example, as a game like "what's in the box." It is important that the blind child understand the use of the sleep shades. That is why I have very rarely used sleep shades with children under 4 years of age for cane travel. In addition, I have found particular success using sleep shades with blind children with partial sight who had attention deficit disorder. Without the distraction of vision, these children have been better able to attend to their touch and sound information and make a more efficient plan for orientation and mobility. Without the sleep shades, these children would often go where they could see, as their vision directed them, which was not necessarily the destination of where they wanted to go.

AGE/STAGE APPROPRIATE SKILLS FOR HOME, SCHOOL, AND COMMUNITY

The above list of basic cane and movement skills is a foundation for learning to be a traveler at home, in school, and in the community. With the early introduction to cane travel, exploring with the cane and learning the necessary skills, blind children can learn in an age/stage appropriate manner to be independent travelers.

Below is a list of skills that blind children can and should be able to do independently by the time they finish third or fourth grade level of development. These are everyday tasks at home, school, and community that their sighted peers are performing. Remember that this is a process, so start early in preschool. If you do, the child will be on the way to being an independent traveler. For the following skills listed, *independent* means *without* the use of a sighted/ human guide. This does not mean that the child can never use the sighted/human guide; rather, the child can do these skills without being guided. Doing the skill *solo is the first goal.* Using a guide is an option *after* the skill has been learned. All children are taught and monitored when learning and practicing these basic skills. Monitoring takes the form of verbal questions, prompts, suggestions and reinforcing skills learned. The parents and school staff will be using their teaching canes at times.

Home

- Moves about safely and with an orientation within the home.
- Is familiar with the driveway and how it connects to the street and sidewalk.
- Knows how to get to and from the front and back of the home outdoors.
- Knows how to get to and from any playground equipment in the yard and how to use the equipment.
- Is familiar with getting to the neighbor's house on each side of child's home.
- Knows how to shoreline.
- Can get mail from the mailbox.
- Can walk to the end of the sidewalk or the block to mail a letter at a mailbox.
- Is familiar with the sidewalk and the block where the home is located.
- Can walk to a store located on the same block, make a purchase, and return home.
- Is able to cross the street in front of the home and other nearby streets.
- Can get to a friend's house and back.
- Knows how to tell others about the cane and how it is used to get around independently.

School

- Is oriented to the classroom.
- Walks independently in the hallway.

- Can perform line walking with classmates in the beginning, middle, or end of the line.
- Goes up and down steps independently.
- Handles lunch time (carrying a tray with a cane and finding a seat in the cafeteria) independently.
- Uses the playground at recess and uses play equipment.
- Goes through doorways, managing the cane, and holding the door for others.
- Uses the bathroom and takes care of personal hygiene needs.
- Walks solo when exiting the school in a fire drill and understands safety procedures.
- Takes messages to the office.
- Gets to and from the school bus, enters and exits the bus, takes a seat, manages the cane on the bus, and understands the emergency routine on the bus.
- Takes a seat in the auditorium, walks up and down the isle, gets on and off the stage.
- Knows how to tell others about the cane and how it is used for getting around independently.

Community

- Accompanies family to local playgrounds, parks and places of worship.
- Becomes familiar with the environment in these community settings.
- Makes purchases at stores.
- Accompanies family to the supermarket and walks along using cane to navigate up and down the isles; gradually learns to orient to entering and exiting the store and where the cashiers are located.
- Walks alongside parents in parking lots going to and from the family car.

- Becoming familiar with mass transportation by taking rides on planes, trains, buses, and so on.
- Can find a favorite store at a mall by gathering information.
- Leads the way in familiar community environments, telling parents the information being used to get to the destination.
- Knows how to tell others in the community about the cane and how it is needed for getting around independently.

This is just a basic list of important skills and gives direction on where to focus when thinking about the home, school, and community in the daily living routine. I have known blind students, totally and partially sighted, in junior and senior high school who have not been able to do these tasks independently. This supports the premise that it's not how much vision the students have that matters or that through maturation *alone* blind children will learn the necessary skills in an incidental manner, rather it attests to the fact that what matters is how many nonvisual *independent movement and travel skills they possess*. Therefore, use this list as somewhat of a functional assessment of skills that should be in place by the end of third or, at the latest, forth grade level of development.

Some of these skills can be expected from blind children in the preschool years. If the child has a developmental delay, then the child should be performing at the developmental stage. If the child's developmental level is under 3 years of age, then use a developmental scale for children birth to three as a guide to what skills babies learn and what the goals can be, then add the alternative skills needed for the blind child to be age/stage appropriate.

Cane travel for blind children from the bottom-up works best when the parents, O&M professional service providers and school staff collaborate to provide adequate service, instruction and practice of independent movement and travel skills that are age/stage appropriate. The O&M specialist should be the catalyst to initiate this process toward independence.

If the O&M professional does not assume this role, then parents must promote the independent movement and travel of their child at home and in the school. And if the parent does not assume this role, then school staff must become informed and initiate the O&M interests of the child. If the school does not, then who is left to promote such independence in the child? Adults can advocate for themselves but young blind children cannot. Adults, parents, blindness professional service providers, and school staff must recognize their responsibilities to facilitate and promote the independent movement and travel in blind children.

The Promotion Model for the independent movement and travel of blind children is not an abstract concept. It is based on experiences of the lives of blind children. It must live, breathe and grow as blind children do. We adults must be committed to the children in our promises for their future by taking responsibilities in the present, in the day-to-day interactions with them. The future of blind children is *more* than a promise of a hopeful future of independence. For in the words of JA Spender, "it is cheap generosity which promises the future in compensation for the present." The future is promised by learning the skills of blindness. This is done by the blind child receiving adequate and appropriate age/stage instruction in the skills of blindness.

CHAPTER 5

INDEPENDENT MOVEMENT AND TRAVEL

A Pictorial Guide

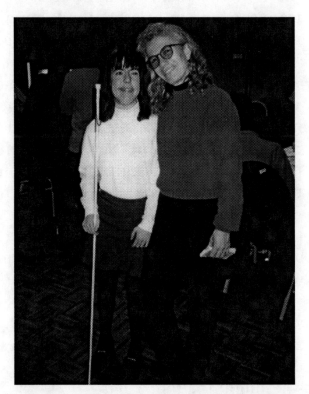

From the time she was a baby until the day she entered college,
I have had the privilege of contributing to the process of
independence for Carol Castellano's daughter, Serena.

Independent Movement and Travel in Blind Children: A Promotion Model, pp. 193–303
Copyright © 2007 by Information Age Publishing
All rights of reproduction in any form reserved.

> *Some of us, observing that ideals are rarely achieved, proceed to the
> error of considering them worthless. Such an error is harmful.
> True North cannot be reached either, since it is an abstraction,
> but it is of enormous importance, as all the world's travelers can attest.*
>
> —Steve Allen

The Promotion Model stresses the assets of blind children to encourage independent movement and travel. This approach is an alternative to conventional orientation and mobility (O&M) and is based on normal child development and the nonvisual skills of blindness. This chapter illustrates, from the bottom-up, that the Promotion Model for independent movement and travel *is a process toward independence.*

The pictorial guide in this chapter gives a concrete testimonial for what some of these skills look like and what can be said about them. All photos are labeled and the action described and discussed. This developmental pictorial guide can provide you with a more intimate understanding of what blind children require in order to develop independent movement and travel. Indeed, I taught the majority of children in these photos. Also included are photos of blind adults who are mentors and professional service providers for the blind. And, of course, there are photos of parents and other educators who share the developmental journey with blind children.

This developmental guide in photos illustrates the *building blocks* of the Promotion Model outlined in chapter 1. The photos highlight the following:

- The parent's role as the child's first O&M teacher;
- The importance of the components of movement to acquiring early motor milestones;
- The need for exploration as an active mover and traveler;

- The early start to cane travel and the "teaching cane";
- The longer cane approach to travel;
- The use of sleep shades;
- The developmental considerations for basic cane skills;
- The approaches to use with developmentally delayed and/or multiple disabled blind children;
- The importance of role release with the parent and school staff; and
- The mentoring of blind children as they transition into youth and adulthood.

The developmentally delayed or multiple disabled blind child is not placed as a separate category of blind children but rather interwoven in this guide at the age/stage appropriate level. If you think of this developmental outline of early childhood O&M like the growth of a tree, the strong roots are the philosophy and principles and the trunk of the tree is the developmental perspectives that fuel and, along with the roots, form its structure. The branches are the strategies that provide the direction of the growth for the tree. The leaves and flowers are the practices and techniques that nurture and bloom and express the individuality of the tree. The additional needs of developmentally delayed or multiple disabled children will necessitate more branching out of the tree.

Overall, I hope that this pictorial guide will raise your level of expectations for the independent movement and travel of blind children. These children are our teachers and offer us a window onto how they need to learn. If we observe the children carefully and are informed about the many possibilities with which we can set the stage for and engage unobtrusively in their development, then the outcome will be confident children on the road to independence.

INDEPENDENT MOVEMENT AND TRAVEL: A PROCESS TOWARD INDEPENDENCE

1.   The Premature Baby

Description: Some babies get off to an early start. This baby is being held by her mother and was born premature at 23 and a half weeks gestation.

After more than 4 months in the hospital, the baby is almost ready to go home. Some babies born this premature have even longer hospital stays before they can go home. In addition to blindness, babies born this premature are at risk of having developmental delays that may be mild, moderate, or severe in nature. The misconceptions about blindness in itself causing delays can cloud the real issue for the child's developmental delay. A clear understanding of positive age/stage appropriate expectations is needed first so that parents and professional service providers can understand and address the child's other needs, delays, or additional disabilities that can accompany severe premature birth. Prematurity and the need for adjustment of developmental age versus chronological age are discussed in chapters 1, 2, and 3.

2.   Face to Face: The Voice-Face Event

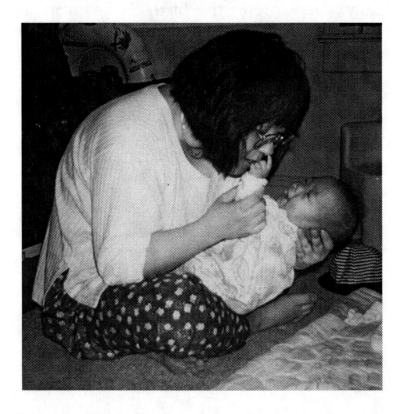

Description: This mother and baby are experiencing each other face to face. The mother is linking touch and sound together in what can be described as the voice-face event. She is gently guiding the arm of her baby to contact her face. When this blind baby hears the mother's voice, she can experience the touch of the mother's face. This interaction produces a smile on the baby's face.

This is an example of an *alternative skill* of blindness; the baby can not experience her mother with vision but can experience, recognize, and enjoy her using touch. Remember that in the early development of all babies, sound has very little meaning unless verified by vision and/ or touch. The sighted child will verify sound primarily with vision and the blind child will verify sound with touch. Chapter 2 discusses furnishing the midline space— activities to make the chest area an interesting place.

3. Midline Play

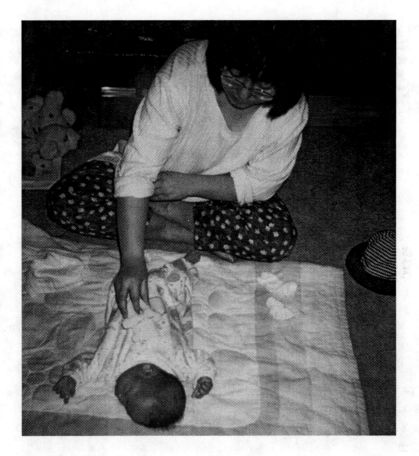

Description: As the baby lies on her back, the mother stimulates the midline (chest/stomach) area of her body. This touch information stimulates curiosity that the baby will respond to by bringing her hands to the center of her body to explore the touch. In this case the mother is using a soft toy that makes sound when moved.

This is an example of on body contact and exploration with the hands, which all babies, blind and sighted, engage in before reaching off body. Remember that tactile reach is the *precursor* to visual reach in all sighted babies and the precursor to auditory reach in blind babies. Reaching and searching are discussed in chapter 2.

4.   Mother and Baby Playing Together

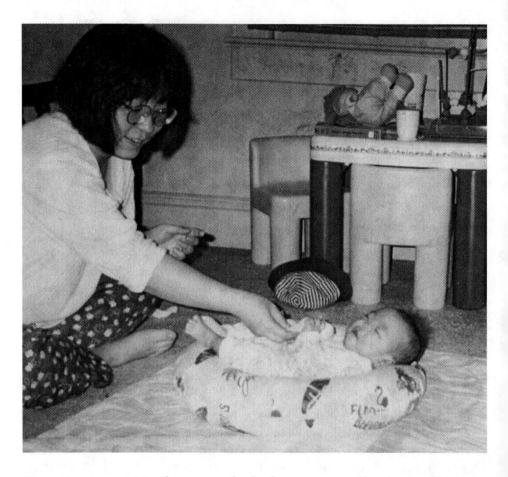

Description: Mother and baby are enjoying playing together using a baby-sized inner tube. Here the baby rests in the tube on her back. The structure of the inner tube brings the hands of the baby to midline and invites the baby to play with the toy the mother is offering.

This is an alternative skill of an *"environmental intervention,"* meaning the structure and function of the object affords an opportunity for the hands to explore at midline. The inner tube has many possibilities for play and movement. The parent, the baby's physical therapist from an early intervention program and I came up with activities to do in the inner tube that would facilitate the components of movement. Such inner tubes can be used with the baby on the stomach as well. The baby can also lay over one side of the inner tube with the upper trunk propped up; toys can be placed in the center of the inner tube. Also, the baby might be able to push the tube since it is easy to slide. The parent as the child's first teacher is discussed in chapters 1 through 4.

5.   The Mother's Lap as the First Classroom

Description: The mother is sitting on the floor with her legs somewhat crossed and the baby is supported in a sitting position on her lap. With the *mother's lap as the first classroom*, the baby is enjoying playing with her mother's hands and listening to her sing. The baby is sitting with her back toward her mother and they are both "looking" in the same direction.

In this position the mother can move in different ways and the baby can experience the same movement: sitting, weight shifting, and hip rotation. For example, the baby may move over to the side and then on her stomach over the mother's knee. This would invite other movements in this position. The parent is the *first ground* for the baby. As an alternative technique, when parents are lying on their backs on the floor, the baby can be placed face down on their stomach. The chest and face of the parent become fun areas to explore for the baby. Blind babies will push up on the parent's stomach; this human interaction is much more interesting and presents many more possibilities than the baby on the plain surface of the floor. Chapters 1 and 2 discuss the parents role, particularly as the first ground for the baby.

6.   Playing in an Inner Tube

Description: This occupational therapist has placed the baby into a larger inner tube in a sitting position.

In this way the baby can explore moving forward and sideways but not falling to the floor, as the inner tube prevents this from happening. The baby can accidentally or purposefully move to the side of the inner tube and push off of it. It is easier to upright his body from this position than it would be if he were to go to the floor without the support of the inner tube. Also, it is important to note that the inner tube creates a circular boundary for the child to explore. Items can be attached with Velcro around the tube. This would facilitate exploration and rotation at the hip. Sighted babies have visual preview of their boundaries that provide end points for reaching. Blind babies need the same opportunity. As an alternative, tactile boundaries can provide the preview and end points for reaching too. Chapter 2 discusses more activities with do with babies.

7. "Pat Mat" Play

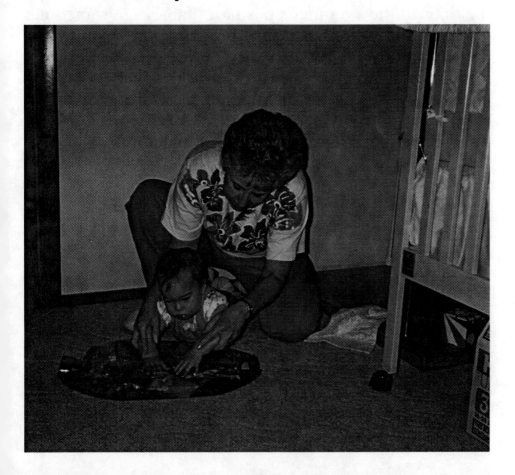

Description: This grandmother is facilitating her grand-child's playing with a "pat mat," which is a heavy rectangu-lar plastic bag filled with water and objects that would interest babies by sight or touch.

When the baby touches the mat, the items in the bag move. Blind babies can enjoy the feeling of the movement of the mat and objects. This baby who was born prema-ture, when on his stomach, would tend to keep his hands behind him in a more infantile "swimmer's position." The physical therapist has suggested that he is ready to explore with his hands in more advanced positions. The grand-mother has gently facilitated the movement of his arms toward the front of him so he can feel the pat mat. This is a more purposeful use of the prone position than to be on the floor in the swimmer's position. Babies can sometimes get *stuck* in positions that may provide more primitive or immature movements than they are capable of performing. By facilitating the arms forward, this baby is capable of playing with the toy at a higher level of motor movement and control. Chapters 2 and 3 discuss activities for blind babies born full term or born premature.

8. Play With an Adapted Toy

Description: This child is developmentally delayed and is learning the possibilities of the prone position with an adapted toy. His arm is connected to the toy, so when he moves his arm it activates the toy and creates a *cause and effect* connection. When the toy makes a sound, operates a fan, or makes some other response to his arm movement, he would enjoy it. This resulted in moving his arm again to produce the effect.

There are many adapted toys on the market that can be initiated by a switch, a plate, a light touch, and a sound. Therapists are usually able to choose a toy *that would be fun* for the child's developmental level and appropriate for the child's components of movement to operate the toy. Chapter 3 discusses activities for the developmentally delayed child and chapter 4 relates Active Learning for the multiple disabled child to the Promotion Model.

9.   Discovering Your Feet

Description: While lying on the couch on his back, this baby is pulling his feet toward his mouth.

This is an important movement pattern for all babies. It is interesting to note that in this position the baby is being introduced to the "sitting position" while lying on his back. The components of movement that are involved in bringing the feet to the mouth will be the foundation for sitting when the baby is ready for this position. Chapter 2 discusses the progressions in child development and the components of movement necessary for the child to develop quality movement of the hands and feet.

10. Playing on the Floor

Description: This child is in a natural play space on a hardwood floor in her home. Objects that are rich in resonance have been placed near her so that she can play with them. She is enjoying an empty gift wrap cylinder and the echo it provides. By her side is a coffee can with some coffee beans in it and a push toy that makes popping sounds when moved. The play space is located near a corner of the room to add the echo effect.

This is an example of an echolocation play space discussed in chapter 2.

11.   Tunnel-Barrel-Drum (Barrel) Play

Description: This baby is inside a tunnel-barrel-drum sitting upright. The barrel is placed on its side with both
ends open. This play space affords a wonderful echo and
resonance and this little girl can move the barrel from side
to side controlling the speed of movement. She has a tam-
bourine in one hand and is controlling the movement of
the barrel with the other hand by pushing her hand strate-
gically on the inside surface of the barrel.

For children who are not ready to control the movement, place pillows or other objects next to the outside of
the barrel to prevent movement at first and gradually—
inch by inch—move the pillows further away. The barrel is
very good for accentuating resonance and echolocation
play. It affords not only tactile boundaries but auditory
boundaries as well. Echolocation and resonance play activities are discussed in chapter 2.

12. "Little Room"

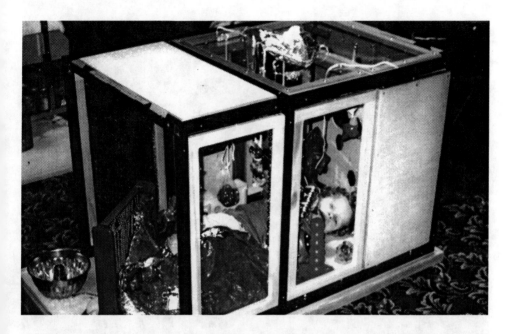

Description: This is the Little Room with a child inside exploring the different objects that are suspended from the top. The Little Room is placed on the Resonance Board that affords vibration, tactile, and resonance information.

As the child moves the legs, hands, and parts of the body, objects are contacted and stimulate curiosity and exploration. The richness of the tactile and sound space created by the Little Room are a great source of self-amusement. Because part of the Little Room is constructed with a transparent material, the child can be visually observed by the sighted adult, and because it is so rich in resonance, the child can be observed through the auditory channel by the blind adult. Photos 13 to 16 illustrate other materials developed by Dr. Nielsen, all of which are discussed in greater detail in chapter 3.

13. "Support Bench"

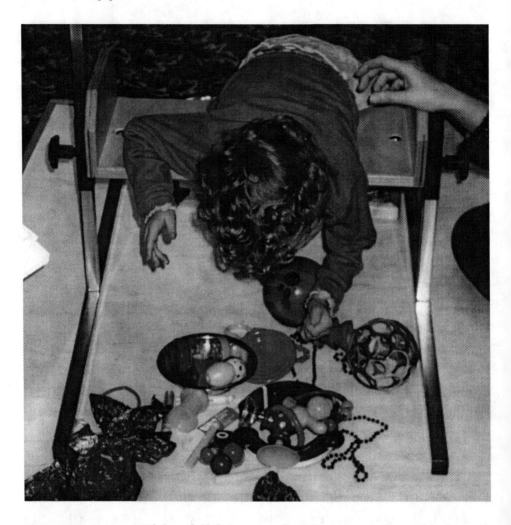

Description: This child is on the Support Bench that is placed over the Resonance Board. Objects are placed on the board for the child to contact with hands and feet.

Simultaneous movement of the hands and feet are needed for more advanced locomotion as the child develops. Some of the components of movement for crawling are facilitated by the use of the Support Bench. It can be raised or lowered depending on the child's size, reach, or ability. A parent is nearby unobtrusively available to the child. Chapter 2 discusses the components of movement for motor development of the child.

14.   "HOPSA Dress"

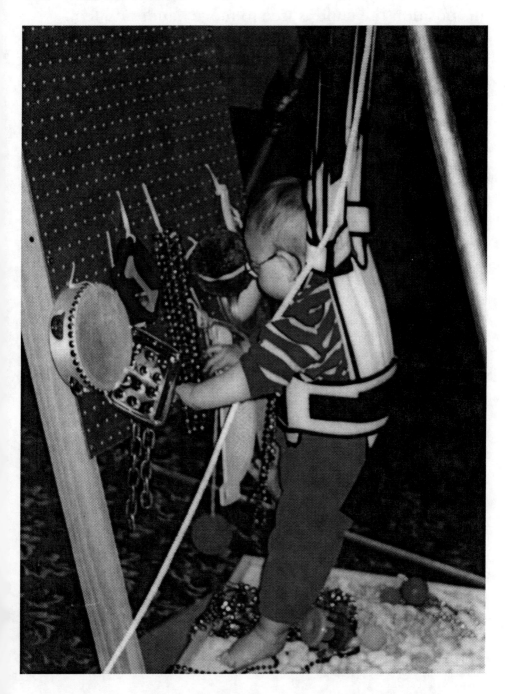

Description: This child is in a HOPSA Dress, which permits free movement of the legs. She can contact objects on the Resonance Board with her feet. Objects placed in front of her on a pegboard can be contacted with her hands. In this position the child is free to move hands and feet.

While she is in the upright position, the child can explore as her interest and developmental level motivate her to do so. The amount of contact with the Resonance Board and suspension of the HOPSA Dress is carefully thought out, depending on muscle strength and other factors of the child's development. This HOPSA Dress facilitates movement components that can only be developed if the child is in a relaxed upright position, for example, stepping motions that the child will eventually make. Dr. Nielsen's philosophy is discussed in chapter 3.

15. "Resonance Board"

Description: This child is enjoying learning on the Resonance Board.

The items chosen for the child to contact and interact with were the result of an assessment of the child's needs and level of development.

Verbal feedback from the adult observer is given at strategic times that do not conflict with the child's own vocalizations or activity. The adult can parallel play with the child. This may be imitating or initiating sounds, responding with like sounds using objects the child is using. The child learns through curiosity stimulated by the resonance and vibration afforded by the Resonance Board. As a result of the characteristics of the Resonance Board, the child responds with interest and motivation. The use of resonance is discussed to varying degrees and for different purposes in each of chapters 1 through 4.

16. "MFA Table"

Description: This child is on the Resonance Board combined with a MFA (Multi-Functional Activities) Table. The table has textured trays and adjustable legs. The adult observer is the executive director of the Lilliworks Active Learning Foundation, Rand Wrobel.

The MFA Table permits the child, who can sit or kneel, possibilities for engaging with objects in different positions, thereby using different motor components of movement. Active movement is facilitated due to the structure and function of this table.

17.   Beginning to Crawl Toward Sound

Description: The blind baby here is beginning to crawl toward a sound source as she leaves the space of the professional service provider.

Once the blind baby has developed on body contact then, like all babies, she will reach off body to a sound. It is important that the sound source be familiar to the baby. Sighted babies use vision and touch and blind babies use sound and touch. Touch verification and identification of the object or person is needed before the sound can become a meaningful motivation to reach off body. The development of reaching is discussed more extensively in chapter 2.

18.   Blind Baby Crawling to Her Father

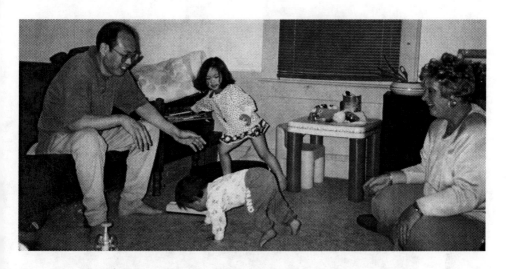

Description: Here the same baby is crawling to her father as her sister looks on.

She is also beginning to elevate herself in the crawl position to get ready to stand as she hears her father's voice getting closer. There is nothing quite like the lure of the parent's voice in motivating their child to move and make contact with them. Remember, from the Promotion Model point of view, person permanence is the precursor to object permanence. This means that in typical development, all sighted and blind babies will search out the parent before searching out an object without a visual, sound, or touch clue. Object permanence and the markers for it are discussed in chapter 2.

19.   Adapted Crawling Activity

Description: This child is learning to crawl but often loses muscle strength and falls from a four-point position to the floor. An alternative approach is demonstrated by the early intervention specialist who is using a piece of cloth that she has placed under the child's stomach and holds in her hands. In this way, should the child start to lose balance, the interventionist can pull up on the cloth to support the child.

This strategy may not be appropriate across the board for blind children, but it may be valuable for children who have difficulty maintaining a crawl position due to other factors impacting their development. This child knew that the cloth support was good and it facilitated the duration of her crawling and developing muscle strength. This activity increased the child's success and therefore sustained her interest in crawling. The role of crawling in developing the components of movement for the child is discussed in chapter 2.

20. Pulling to Stand

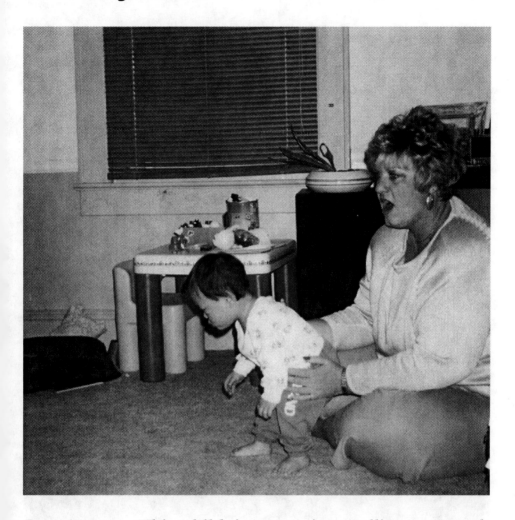

Description: This child is mastering pulling to stand, which is one of the last skills achieved before walking independently. She gradually receives less and less support by the adult who is unobtrusively available for verbal or tactile prompts only when needed to facilitate movement.

Many blind children can maintain standing alone but have not learned the components of movement to get themselves to stand; these children are often lifted up to the standing position by adults. Further discussion on the components of movement and transition from standing to walking are discussed in chapter 2.

21.   First Steps

Description: The same child has mastered pulling to stand, standing alone, and cruising along furniture and walls and is ready to walk. In this photo she hears her dad's voice and walks to him. Then as he moves slowly about making snapping sounds with his fingers and singing, his daughter turns and moves toward him to find him and receive a big hug.

This is an example of keeping near the child for an attunement. Because the baby can't see the parent and the sound of the parent in another room may not be a motivator at this time in her development, by being closer to the child she is motivated to go to her dad. The role of additional touch and closer proximity to the blind child is discussed in chapters 1 through 4.

22.   Playing With Push Toys

Description: This baby has just learned to walk and is enjoying climbing on her little car push toy. She will climb over on her own and sit on the car and push it to move with her feet. When the car is weighted down on the seat with a large bag of rice, she enjoys standing, moving forward, and pushing it around the room. This is one of the many push toys that babies will use.

These common push toys on the market allow blind children, like sighted children, to learn to push and experience moving about their world in a manner that is fun. This promotes exploration and learning. Push toys are a more natural way for children to explore rather than the precane. I have found that one of the most enjoyable push toys is the Hula-Hoop, as it can be used in so many ways—solo by the child or with the parent. Push toys can often be used around the same time as the blind child is being introduced to the cane. Such a mobility device is preferable to the formalized precanes discussed in chapter 4.

23.   Table From Conductive Education

Description: This child has pulled independently to stand from a seated position with the use of this unique table.

The concept for this table comes from Conductive Education in Hungary. Conductive Education places a prime emphasis on the functional movement of the child. In this photo the child has pulled to stand and can move around the table by holding on to the slots of wood on its top. Once the child has finished exploring, she can return to her seat, hold on to the table and sit down. This is another example of structure and function facilitating the active movement of the child. See the Resource chapter for more information regarding Conductive Education. The characteristics of the play equipment and intervention for children are discussed in each chapter.

24. "Ladder-Back" Chair From Conductive Education

Description: This is another wooden educational tool used in Conductive Education. In this photo the teacher is facilitating movement by pushing the ladder lightly forward while standing behind the child. This creates the initial momentum the child needs to get the ladder going.

Here the child holds on to the ladder at the height that is functional for her. The child can push the ladder for functional mobility around the classroom. This concept of a moveable ladder is used in Conductive Education by attaching a ladder to the back of a chair, thus creating a "ladder-back" chair. The child, therefore, can get up from a seated position, move around to the back of the chair, push it to the desired destination, and sit down in the chair. The child can do this entire process independently. Facilitating active movement is discussed in each chapter, developmentally from early motor development to use of the cane for travel.

25. Learning About Steps

Description: This blind toddler is learning to go up and down steps. This child is learning how to navigate the "ups and downs" of steps, where they lead, the boundaries at the sides of them, what they are composed of and what covers them.

This is a vital skill for *all* children yet adults often keep blind children away from steps at a developmentally appropriate time due to a fear that they will fall. It is important to note that many of the same components of movement used in crawling are also used to go up and down steps. Therefore, blind children who are delayed in crawling may benefit greatly by exploring steps. The significance for active movement, of exposing the blind child to exploring and becoming independent on steps, can not be overstated. Some ideas for exploring steps are discussed in chapter 2.

26.   Enjoying the Tyke Bike

Description: This toddler is enjoying her tyke bike. She is pushing off the grass with her foot to get back on the sidewalk.

Through this typical toddler play activity, she is learning about staying on a sidewalk, maintaining a straight line of direction, the width of the sidewalk, and the boundaries on both sides. Therefore, when the child uses her cane, the information from the *tip of the cane* will have more meaning because she has experienced "sidewalkness" with her gross motor movements on the tyke bike. Age/stage appropriate activities for independent movement and travel are discussed in each chapter.

27.   Using a "Walker" to Facilitate Walking

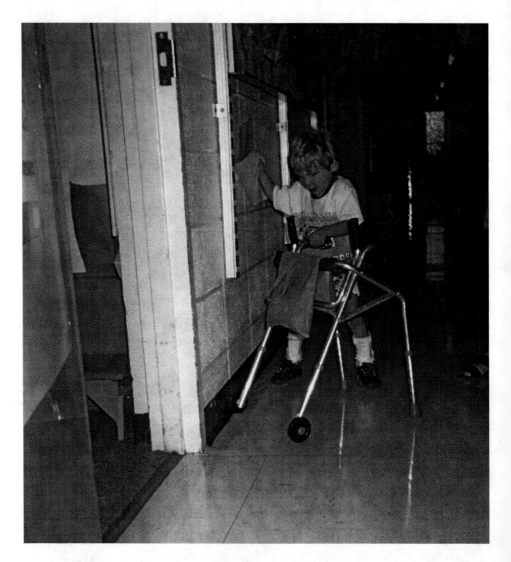

Description: This child is using a "walker" during occupational therapy time to meet his drive to move and need to know and become a traveler in the world. The occupational therapist has included getting to the classroom as part of the therapy session. In addition, in this photo the child has moved toward the wall, which he has heard through the use of echolocation. From here he can transition from the walker to the wall for exploring. Eventually, he will return to his walker and continue going down the hall.

For some children I have attached the cane to the walker with Velcro. When the child gets to the wall, he can pull the cane from the walker and use it to explore the wall, facilitating exploring and movement. When he gets back to the walker, the cane can be reattached and the child can be on his way again. Various approaches to use with children with development delays are discussed further in Chapters 3 and 4.

28.   Taking First Steps With a Cane Independently

Description: This is the same child who was using the walker and is now taking his first steps in open space with a cane. Before working with him I had thought that blind children would be exposed to the cane only *after* they learned to walk. This child was delayed in walking and had reached the stage with his walker that he had all the components of movement necessary for walking but had not taken steps in an open space on his own. I had tried precane devices with this child but he could not use them. The combination of their weight and his leaning forward caused him to lose balance. I consulted with the parent, classroom teacher and therapists and we agreed to give the cane a try. Home and school introduced the cane and the child experimented in both settings using it. Within a couple of weeks this child took his *first* steps across an open space with the cane.

What he needed was more *information,* not support from the walker or adult's hand. The cane provided him this information, forming a tripod of information with his two feet. This experience caused me to rethink my protocols regarding initiating the cane with the blind child. The developmentally delayed or multiple disabled blind child needs the same advantages as the typically developing blind child when learning to use the cane. From working with this one child I began to explore the use of the cane with a variety of children who were delayed in development and not walking. See chapter 3 for information regarding developmentally delayed or multiple disabled blind children. See chapter 4 for issues and concerns regarding precane devices.

29. Mother Using Her Teaching Cane

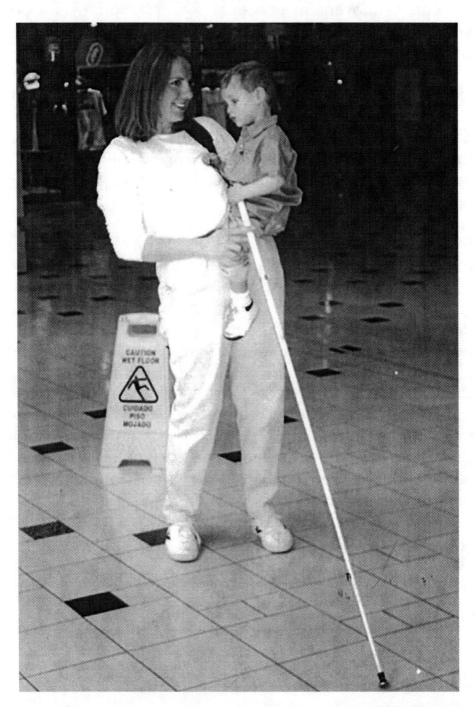

Description: This mother is holding and tapping her "teaching cane" and her son, who has recently learned to walk, has reached out to feel what she is holding and make the tapping sound for himself. The mother can then place the child on the floor where he can further explore movement with the cane as the parent holds the cane at the grip end. He can manipulate the cane and tap it himself. This is one of the most important advantages of the longer cane approach to travel: the child and the parent can both hold onto the cane for a *shared* travel experience.

Role releasing the use of the teaching cane to parents is a very important part of the bottom-up approach to learning how to use the cane. Children learn many life skills from their parents and the use of the cane should be one of them. Role release is presented in chapter 1 and discussed in different ways in chapters 2 through 4.

30.   O&M Instructor Using the Teaching Cane

Description: In this photo the same child is holding onto my teaching cane. He is guiding my cane as we walk, he in front and me behind. In my other hand is the child's cane that he is familiar with and will use later in the lesson.

When possible, I always have the parents introduce the cane to the child first. The parents have *their* teaching cane and I, as the O&M specialist, have mine. This is part of the *role release* process in which the parent is the blind child's first O&M teacher. Sometimes the child holds both canes, one in each hand, comparing the difference. Remember, for children, toys are their tools too. The opportunities for developmental guidance with the teaching cane are many. It is the most natural, bottom-up experience for the blind child to walk with an adult using the teaching cane. See chapter 4 for more information about the teaching cane.

31.   Learning to use the Cane for the First Time

Description: This is a photo of a child with the parent learning to use the longer cane approach to travel for the first time. The smile on the child's face tells the story.

The child begins to explore by letting go of the parent's hand and taking an interest in what is being held in the hand. The cane is a tool for intelligent use facilitating exploration and navigation in the environment. The child is getting connected to the cane by receiving information about the environment. Chapter 4 discusses first time cane use by the child.

32. Learning About Information From the Cane via the O&M Specialist and Role Release to the Parent

Description: I am talking to a child about the differences in the tiles on the floor that he felt with his cane. With the metal tip cane he could discriminate between the different shapes of the tiles and textures and he was curious to take a closer look with his hands. The child's father and sister are watching nearby. Alongside me on the floor is my teaching cane. After a little modeling of how the teaching cane can be used, I will next equip the father with the teaching cane too, and then the father and son will go on a mall walk together.

The mall is an excellent place for cane travel with blind babies, toddlers, and preschoolers. The flat, level, and wide-open space permits movement possibilities that the home and school don't usually offer. Using a metal tip cane, the child can learn to detect changes in floor surfaces, such as differences in tile patterns and the texture and edges of carpeting. Hallways, the recessed doorways of stores, closures, and openings in the architecture of the mall, create echo spaces that invite the child to explore. The metal tip cane is superior to plastic tip canes for getting echo and resonance information, as well as for gaining vibrations and tactile feedback from the floor surfaces. Chapter 4 discusses more about the characteristics of the cane to consider for blind children.

33. Walking Down the Driveway

Description: This preschool child is going to the mail-box, which is at the end of his driveway. His mother is looking on from a distance.

Once the child has learned to move independently from the parent, when using the cane, the child can learn to move to destinations around the outside of the home that are meaningful. Mastering the outdoor home environ-ment is important for all children. Chapter 4 lists various skills in home, school, and community that the child will be able to accomplish by third grade.

34.   Going Down the Laundry Steps With the Cane

Description: This child is learning to go down the laundry steps. These are steps made for a laundry cart, narrow with a ramp on each side for the wheels of the cart. This traveler is exploring the ramp part of the stairway with her mother monitoring her movement, as would any parent of a toddler learning a new skill. She is learning to hold onto the railing and use her cane to preview the downward slope of the ramp. Unfortunately, because the number of photos for this book had to be limited, I could not show you the fun she had with exploring the washer and dryer.

When the blind child learns to use the cane first in the home environment, there are a variety of places and situations to explore. This facilitates learning and generalizing the use of the cane in a *natural everyday* manner. Discussion of what initial cane travel will look like and the different interventions and practices to use with the first time cane traveler is presented in chapter 4.

35.   Roller Skating With the Cane

Description: This is the same child as in previous photo
and here she is on roller skates while her mom watches
closely.

The cane can be used in a variety of ways to assist a new
skill. For example, before she learned to skate with her
cane in front of her, down on the ground clearing her
path, her mother held the cane horizontally out in front of
her and the child held onto to cane and was guided to get
the feeling of the motion. Gradually, as she was able to
maintain balance, she gripped the cane as a travel tool.
Blind children will want to have fun with their cane as a
tool that facilitates playing in the world. Sighted children
have their vision to facilitate having fun and blind children
have their cane. Chapter 4 discusses the bottom-up,
exploring, and self-amusement that learning the cane provides the blind child.

36. Cane Walk with Father

Description: This preschooler is out for a walk with his father to explore and learn about using the cane. The child locates a puddle with his cane. Like all children, he wants to go splash in the puddle, but, for the time being, splashing with the cane will do. This father enjoyed taking cane walks with his son. It was their special time together and the father was very proud of his son's accomplishments as an independent traveler.

It is very important for fathers to become involved in the play and everyday skill learning of blind children. The learning of the long cane often gives fathers an opportunity to engage with their child in skill development. In my experience as an itinerant O&M specialist, most of my contacts at home were with mothers, as the fathers were usually working. Sometimes fathers would take off from work to be home for the consult as well or meet me at school to observe a lesson. Both parents play vital roles in the development of their child. As discussed in chapter 1, the teaching cane is a tool that can bring families together for learning and active engagement.

37. Using the Cane on Playground Equipment

Description: This is the same child as in the previous photo now on the neighborhood playground at the jungle gym. This boy had very limited partial sight and could not see that the bars of the climbing apparatus went way above his head. With the cane, however, he could explore for information, affording him to climb higher.

This creative use of the cane is another example of the longer cane approach to travel. The cane is a tool that *gathers information* and facilitates choices and decision making on the part of the child. As the child becomes more proficient in managing the cane, the parent is less likely to hover over the child. The parent comes to under-stand the benefits of the cane as it can reach further out. It provides more preview and gives the child greater time to react to objects ahead. Chapters 3 and 4 discuss the cane as a low vision aid.

38.   Using the Cane on the Balance Beam

Description: This preschool child is learning to walk on a balance beam, an activity the class was doing. Without the cane she would lose her balance. With the cane she was able to walk the entire length of the beam and complete the task as the other children did. Sighted children use their vision to *observe the floor* and this blind child was able to use the cane to get *contact and observation* of the floor.

An alternative approach to get the same task done is what the bottom-up approach is all about. Sighted children have their vision for what they can see and the blind children have their cane for what they can't see. Many partially sighted children benefit from using a cane. Chapter 3 discusses succeeding with partial sight by using the cane. Also, chapter 4 discusses the function of the cane for preview of the environment.

39. Exploring the Preschool Class With the Cane

Description: In the early states of exploring her pre-school class, this child was very tentative to move independently. With the cane she would walk about and explore her class, like the other preschoolers.

The cane is a *contact tool*. It is meant to *touch the world*. Blind children *need to touch the world and all the "stuff" in it*. This is discovery learning. Blind children are not "little adults" who can have the world explained to them without touching it. They can not learn about the world by moving in a vacuum from point A to point B. When being *guided*, all the child observes is someone else's movement. The bottom-up approach encourages children to learn through their own movement.

40. Line Walking With the Cane

Description: Line walking is a very important skill learned in school and highly valued by classroom teachers. This blind child is walking with his class to the New Jersey Tournament of Champions Day. With one hand he is holding onto a rope. This was what *all the children* in the class were expected to do. But in his other hand was an "Olympic Torch" that the children made and were carrying. It was thought that this child could not carry the torch and the cane at the same time. An easy solution was to tape the torch onto the grip end of the cane. In this way the child could have "his cake and eat it too."

Sometimes the classroom teacher or instructional aide may unnecessarily contact or hold onto the blind child when walking in a hallway, as in this photo. The O&M specialist needs to advocate and advise the school staff that children can be responsible for their own movement. If children know the skill, then they do not need to be physically contacted. This picture demonstrates line walking, but it also illustrates this subtle form of contact and monitoring, which is unnecessary. Blind children will never learn full confidence in their own movement and travel if they think someone is always watching or monitoring them. The children will naturally assume over time that the adult, usually sighted, is responsible for their movement. Each chapter gives a number of examples of blind children taking responsibility for their own movement and how adults can facilitate this independence.

41. Walking to the School Bus

Description: This child is learning to walk to her school bus from her preschool class. The instructional assistant observes the child from a distance. If the child needs a sound clue, she is there to facilitate. Usually the child can gather adequate sound localization information by listening to other children talking and moving and to the noise of the bus engine.

Learning to walk to and get on the bus is a basic every-day skill for all children to learn. It gives children an opportunity to travel in a less structured and more crowded situation. It also gives them an opportunity to learn skills that will be valuable later on when using public transportation—getting to, boarding, taking a seat, and getting off the bus. Chapter 4 lists various skills that are age/stage appropriate for children to learn independent movement and travel.

42.   Arriving at the School Bus

Description: This is the same child arriving at the bus. She has located the curb and will locate the first step and door opening. The instructional aide is closer but still unobtrusive, as the child is in the process of learning this skill. Each skill is a process and requires responsibilities from both the adult and the child. The more the child learns the skill, the less the adult is needed.

The process of learning a new skill typically follows this pattern: I do it for you, then with you, and then you do it alone. Blind children are vulnerable to not completing the task independently because adults often continue to do it for them or with them. This photo is a very clear example of *unobtrusive availability*. Unobtrusive availability is one of the building blocks of the Promotion Model and various examples of it are given in chapters 1 through 4.

43.   Running With the Cane

Description: Running is an activity children enjoying doing, especially on the playground. This child is learning to run freely on a blacktop playground by using his long cane. He can go from one end to the other and check out all four sides.

The freedom to run develops muscle strength and confidence and tests the limits of how fast children can go. The longer cane approach affords a safer experience when running and especially when running fast. Running is an age/stage appropriate activity that all children need to experience. Other examples of daily living skills are given throughout the chapters.

44. Wheel Chair Traveler and Exploring With the Cane

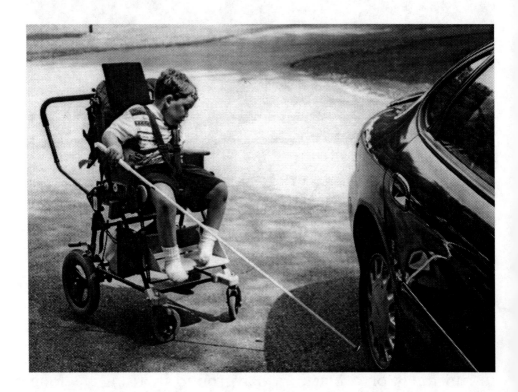

Description: This child is exploring a blacktop area of a parking lot. He is using his wheelchair to get close to the car and his cane to check it out. He has limited residual vision of the type that could miss the car altogether but his cane locates the tire and gives him the opportunity to see the car visually as he moves in closer and checks it out with his hands.

For a wheelchair user, the cane should be long enough for outdoor and indoor use: to touch the street while still on the sidewalk and to detect a drop-off in front or to the side, such as a step down. The initial appearance of the length of this cane may look too long. Once we *realize* the functional skill that the child will be doing independently with it, then this longer length is understood as appropriate. The best set-up for a wheelchair traveler is when one hand is driving the motorized wheelchair so that the other is free to hold the cane. Chapter 4 discusses other variations of using the cane.

45.   Approaching Steps With the Cane

Description: This child is on a landing that approaches a stairway at school. She has learned to move safely and efficiently about her elementary school, so gradually her instructional assistant moves further away and will not be accompanying her at all. In short, once proficient in her travel skills, this blind child will require no more supervision getting around the school than her sighted peers would require.

Sometimes school personnel think they are making it safe for the blind child to go up and down stairs with a classmate, regardless of whether the blind child has a cane. This is one sure way to entertain an accident, as the sighted child and blind child do not necessarily read each other's body language in the same way. For children who are often guided it only seems logical that they would need to be guided on steps as well. It is safer for a blind child to go up or down steps without a cane, simply holding on to the railing, than to hold on to another child. Of course, the safest solution is for the blind child to have and use the cane to manage stairs. Chapter 4 discusses the proper technique for using the cane on stairs.

46.   Going Through the Doorway

Description: In this photo the child is going from inside through a heavy metal door. She has learned to move herself away as she gives that last push so she can clear the door as it closes.

This is another basic skill that blind children must learn: opening, going through, and closing doors without harming themselves or others. Often blind children approach a door and an adult or student opens the door for them. If the "door opener" remains silent, the blind child will not know the location of the door. It is best to let the child approach the door and learn to handle the door independently. There are many types of door handles and blind children will only learn to deal with the various types if they have opportunities to open and close them. One sure way to introduce doors to the blind child is to make the child the door monitor. Chapter 4 lists skills the child will do with appropriate instruction in school and underscores the need for unobtrusive availability.

47. Going Down Steps

Description: This preschooler is going down steps using the longer cane approach to travel.

Blind children will often position the cane closer to the hip and not out in front for maximum protection. The longer cane compensates for this lack of extension. The cane still reaches the next step for the child to give adequate information. With the shorter cane approach, the child will sometimes have the cane on the same step, which can be unsafe. In addition, they are not getting adequate preview and protection of what is ahead. The skill for going down steps is discussed in chapter 4.

48. Locating the Classroom

Description: This kindergarten child was walking in the middle of the hall and has now moved to the wall to locate her classroom. By holding her cane in the hand furthest from the wall she can get protection across her body with the cane. The door to her classroom is open all the way, leaving several inches between it and the wall. If she had the cane in the hand closest to the wall and simply following it, she could miss the door and hit her body or head. However, due to the angle of her cane across her body and the longer cane approach to travel, she manages to contact the open door and will easily go around it into her classroom.

Since independent movement and travel is a process acquired over time, the blind child is placed at an advantage by using a longer cane, which not only gives greater preview but affords more reaction time when contacting objects in the environment. Having more time to react and plan movements facilitates safety and confidence in travel. Chapter 4 discusses the longer cane approach to travel and the use of the cane to locate destinations.

49. Finding a Potential Hazard with the Cane

Description: The post in between two open doors can be a hazard for any child, and even more so for a blind child. The child in this photo is using her cane to avoid such a bump and possible serious injury to her head.

A partially sighted child who does not use a cane or only uses it for identification, and has not been taught to use it purposefully for travel situations, is vulnerable in this situation. I know of many partially sighted children who have had lumps on their head from walking into these posts because they were not using a cane. The use of the cane for partially sighted children is discussed in chapters 3 and 4.

50. Support Cane Used With Travel Cane

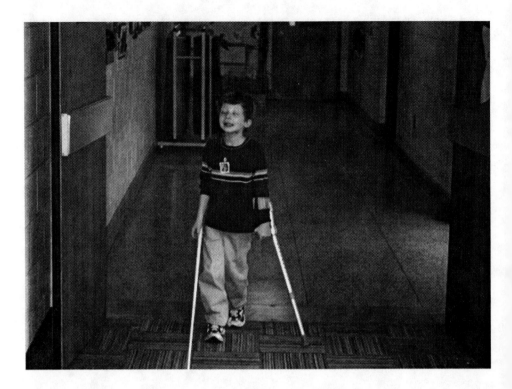

Description: Some blind children may need a support cane, not because of blindness, but because of some other factor that impacts their balance while walking. This photo demonstrates the easy solution to the balance issue of a child with cerebral palsy. The child holds the support cane in one hand and the long cane in the other. Adults in this child's life have promoted the two-cane approach for him to use and be safe traveling in the school environment.

The travel cane is not for support but for detection, protection, information and identification. When this blind child is coming down a hallway using his cane, he is sending the message to the oncoming students and staff of the school: "this is how much space I need to travel safely, so please walk around." Without the cane, this child may not be perceived as blind and students passing by may cross his path quickly and unexpectedly, which causes encounters. These encounters are unnecessary but likely for the support cane traveler who does not also use a travel cane. The child with a support cane only is very vulnerable to being knocked off balance and hurt. Chapter 3 discusses various approaches with children with additional disabilities, one of which is to use the support cane with the travel cane for the physically disabled child.

51.   Coming Up the Steps at Home

Description: This young child has learned to navigate her steps at home. Although she has mastered going up and down the steps, as illustrated in this photo, there is a large space before the first down step. This presented a challenge when she was initially learning this skill because she was not sure how far away the first step down would be. So, strips of wood were placed before the first step to "cue"

her that it was very close and to remind her to look for it with her cane.

Sometimes modifying the environment for the young blind child to accomplish a skill is appropriate, if it permits the child to do it independently. Tactile modifications, as on this porch, teach the child to use the cane more effectively. Visual modifications are not recommended for the partially sighted child because they are easily missed. The variables affecting visual efficiency will make the modification less reliable. In addition, the touch modification enhances a skill of blindness (cane travel) as opposed to the visual modification, which adapts the environment to the inefficient use of partial sight. Various examples of how touch can give blind children exact information about where objects are located in space are discussed in each chapter.

52.   Shorelining With the Cane

Description: This child is shorelining, using the cane along the edge created by the grass and sidewalk, to locate an intersecting sidewalk. When she gets to the sidewalk she is looking for, the cane will touch blacktop or cement and not grass. This will be her clue to turn onto that side-walk.

Shorelining with the cane is one of the skills of blindness. Some partially sighted children who do not use a cane shoreline with their feet because their visual efficiency may be compromised by a number of factors. I have also known totally blind children who do not use a cane and who, as teenagers, used their feet as well. Usually these children are with a guide, but there always comes a time when a guide is not available. These children are in harm's way while traveling, even in familiar surroundings, whereas children who have learned cane skills are able to travel safely and effectively. Succeeding with partial sight is discussed in chapter 3.

53. The Use of Sleep Shades

Description: This child is learning to navigate her playground with the use of sleep shades and the longer cane approach to travel. She is getting around the playground safely, feeling the different textures (gravel and grass), identifying the railroad ties and avoiding falling over the other children. Previously, without the sleep shades, she had problems with orientation and interpreting the information her residual vision was telling her. With the sleep shades the information she gathered from touch and sound were clear and guided her reliably. It has been said that a little knowledge is a dangerous thing and sometimes a little vision can be a dangerous thing too.

Learning nonvisual skills with the sleep shades develops a confidence base to movement and travel that can be relied upon once the sleep shades are removed. This child preferred to keep the sleep shades on all the time when she went out on the playground, even after she learned her blindness skills, because she found her travel less confusing and more efficient. With the child in this photo and the next photo, parent permission and understanding was attained before starting with the sleep shades so that follow-up at home could be provided. When introduced in a positive light and with parent involvement, the use of sleep shades can be a powerful tool for sensory skill development, cane travel skills and overall independence in movement and travel. Sleep shades are used to learn the skills of blindness and are discussed in chapter Three.

54. Sleep Shades Eliminate Visual Distraction

Description: This boy was learning basic cane travel skills with sleep shades because his partial sight was not serving him efficiently, indoors or outdoors. Through the use of sleep shades he learned to orient more effectively to his school and paid more attention to outdoor traffic patterns when learning to recover from orientation mistakes in residential travel. By eliminating the weaker sense (vision)

the child is able to fully attend to his touch and sound information and learn to rely upon these senses in a way he never did before.

When used for orientation, the visual sense is used for distance information, directing the traveler where to go. Children with partial sight or residual vision rely on what their vision may be telling them regardless of the reliability of the information. The result is that these children often move in a direction that they "see" even though it may not be where they want to go. When this happens, the distracting vision misleads them. The use of sleep shades solves this distraction variable and replaces the misguiding information with reliable information. Sleep shades are one of the building blocks of the Promotion Model and are discussed in chapters 1 and 3.

55.   Getting on the Bus

Description: The child in this photo is learning to get on the school bus independently. By introducing a small step before the first school bus step, he was able to pull and step up onto the bus by himself. Because he needs to hold onto the handles of the door and door frame, he can not hold his support cane or travel cane at this time.

These skills will be developed once he has mastered getting on and off the school bus by using two hands. Then he will learn how to use only one hand to hold the railing and in the other hand can hold the canes. As the saying goes, "one step at a time." The process of learning daily living skills comes with practice. With practice comes efficiency and proficiency of the skill. Chapter Three discusses the role of adults as facilitators in early intervention and how to limit early interference.

56.   Coming Off the School Bus

Description: This child is coming off the school bus. The last step off the bus is a high step for many children and the cane must be long enough to give adequate information before the child starts the descent.

   With the shorter cane approach to travel, the cane sometimes does not contact the ground without the child leaning forward. In addition, the bus sometimes stops nearer to or further away from the curb. The child is vulnerable to not knowing if it will be one step after getting off the bus or two or three to get to the curb. The longer cane approach enables quick assessment of the situation. Because O&M is a confidence-based skill, why not give children the type of cane and length that will put them at an advantage in their development? Choosing a longer, lighter cane that is flexible, hollow and has a metal tip promotes feelings of security and confidence in the child. Chapter 4 discusses the characteristics of the cane to consider when choosing a cane for the child.

57.   Learning to use the Cane in New Settings

Description: Here the child is enjoying a day at the beach and learning to use the cane in a different setting and without his shoes and orthotics. He is not as confident walking without his supports for his ankles and legs. The instructional assistant has her teaching cane to tap and gives him information where to move his cane.

Blind children, developmentally delayed or not, need to utilize their cane travel skills in a variety of settings. This gives them opportunities to develop confidence in using their cane and travel skills, anywhere and anytime. Chapter 4 lists a number of skills in the home, school, and community that will facilitate generalizing the learning of cane travel skills.

58. Role Releasing and the Teaching Cane

Description: This first grader is learning about the supermarket. In this photo he is carrying an item he picked up from the shelf and is holding his cane. The instructional assistant is following him using her teaching cane too. She is available for information or to answer questions. It is the child's responsibility to get to the cash register and pay for the item.

When doing a lesson I would use my teaching cane and now I have role released to the instructional assistant. Therefore, if there is an instructional assistant involved, that person can be trained in the skills being worked on with the child. That assistant would also have a cane too. This is part of the role release process at school. Role release and the teaching cane are discussed in Chapter 4.

59.   Practicing New Cane Skills

Description: This preschool child is learning to cover more adequately with his cane while walking on the sidewalk. The instructional assistant is walking alongside and making the tapping and sliding sound of the wider coverage he is learning to imitate. The adult is holding the cane in the pencil grip. This is one of the skills of the longer cane approach to travel. Eventually the child will be able to manage the cane in this manner too.

Even though the child is using the cane at home and school to get around, new cane skills need to be practiced. Parents can take cane walks with their child in the neighborhood and community. Parents and professional service providers must promote the understanding that there must be someone in the school who will be assigned the responsibility of learning about the cane so that the blind child can practice in this setting too. In addition to the possibility of instructional assistants, the physical education teacher, occupational or physical therapist, classroom teachers, and lunch aides are all possible candidates to reinforce and practice cane and travel skills with the child. Consider offering training for these staff to teach them about the cane and how to facilitate the goals of cane travel independence. Practicing skills is part of adequate instruction and, as such, is discussed in a variety of ways in each chapter.

60. Around the School on the Outside

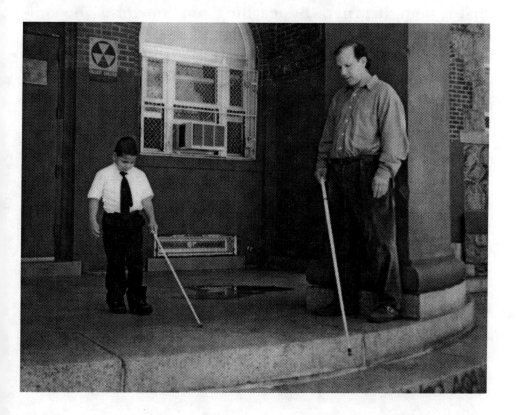

Description: This kindergarten child is learning to get around the outside of his school—from the back door to the front door, the fire drill route, and the location of the playground. This child is using a two-point touch to locate the step drop-off. He is already familiar with sliding his cane and now needs to learn how to lift his cane up in a low arc and tap on each side, one step at a time. This takes practice to build up the confidence for identifying the drop-off of the first step. The instructional assistant is tapping the edge of the step to give a sound cue so that the child has an idea of how close he is getting to the step. Once he gets more confidence in identifying the drop-off, the sound clue will be removed.

This is an example of role release, as the instructional assistant is providing practice of a new skill the student is learning. Sometimes I have the child teach me the skill that is being learned. By teaching someone else, the children demonstrate their knowledge of a skill. So sometimes I will put on sleep shades and have the child teach me the skill. Chapter 4 lists a variety of cane travel skills to learn about the larger environment than just the home or indoors of school.

61. Comparing Canes at Summer Camp

Description: These two children are at a summer camp for blind students. They are comparing two different types of canes. One has a roller ball type tip and is a folding cane of conventional length. The other is a hollow, one piece, lighter, metal tip cane that is longer in length. These two children will be entering first grade in a few weeks after camp ends and already they are using the cane. They are aware of the differences in the canes and are conversing about experiences with their canes. It is the most natural thing for blind children to use canes.

The characteristics of the cane are very important to what the child wants to accomplish with the cane. Some canes offer the blind child advantages and some offer disadvantages. The bottom line is this: *any cane is better than no cane*, but a child should have a cane that is long enough to do the job and light enough to maneuver easily. *The child can always shorten-up on the longer cane, but a shorter cane can not be made longer.* Provide the cane that offers the most advantages and facilitates independent movement and travel. The advantages and disadvantages of different types of canes are presented in chapter 4.

62. Mentoring by the Organized Blind

Description: This photo was taken at a cane walk at the National Federation of the Blind's National Convention a number of years ago. This particular cane walk was with younger children and their parents and a blind travel instructor. The cane walk is sponsored by the National Organization of Parents of Blind Children and is coordinated by the Louisiana Tech O&M Program in Ruston, Louisiana. Blind and sighted travel instructors pair off with blind children, their parents and older first time cane travelers to experience the longer cane approach to travel under sleep shades.

The cane walk is an excellent opportunity for skilled blind adults to mentor blind children and their parents about independent movement and travel skills. Such positive role modeling is the essence of mentoring. Mentoring is discussed in chapter 1 and the importance of positive blind role models is referenced throughout the chapters.

63.   Mentoring Siblings

Description: These three blind children are all from the same family—an older sister and her two brothers. The sister is being a positive role model and mentor to her brothers. Now that she has learned some of the basic cane skills, we are visiting her brothers in another school and she is giving them a cane lesson. The youngest brother is in preschool, the older brother in kindergarten, and the sister in second grade. All three children are using the lighter, longer cane approach for travel.

The older sister is very proud to be teaching her younger brothers what she knows and they are very eager to learn. This is a positive example of using what could be perceived with deficit-thinking about blindness as a problem in a family to have three blind siblings. Instead, it is the most natural thing for these children to be using a cane and be working together as a family to learn the necessary skills to be independent. Remember, we can perceive the child as functional or dysfunctional. Our orientation to blindness and knowledge about the skills of blindness will be the foundation for our perception and practices. Examples of the parent, or in this case the sister, as the blind child's first teacher are given throughout the chapters.

64.   Mentoring Teenagers

Description: The teenagers in this photo are part of a mentoring program called LEAD (Leadership, Education, Advocacy and Determination). Once a month, this mentoring program brings blind teenagers together with skilled blind mentors. It was developed by a partnership with consumers and the state agency servicing the blind. Today's event was going out for lunch and taking a bus to get there. The participants are at the bus stop inquiring whether this is the bus that they want or not. I worked with many of these teenagers when they were young children.

Mentoring is an ongoing process that starts very early in the child's life, first giving hope and positive information about blindness to parents and then giving direct involvement with the child about the possibilities of being an independent traveler. Contact information regarding LEAD can be found in the Resources chapter.

65.   Mentoring a Teenager at a National Convention

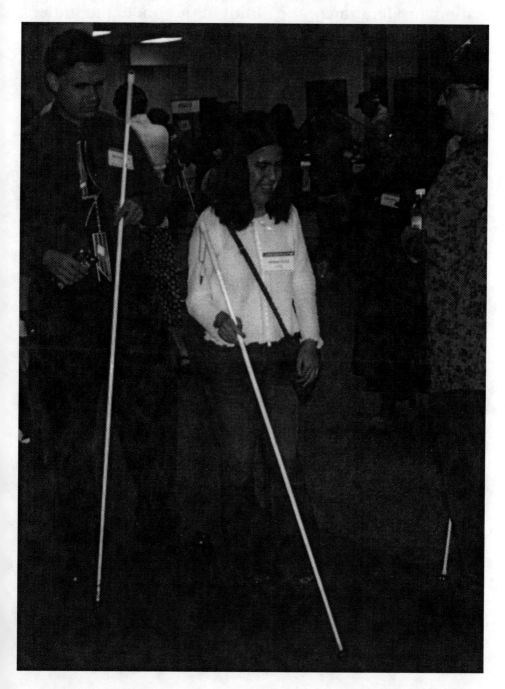

Description: In another example of mentoring, a blind adult from the Louisiana Center for the Blind works with a student in their summer program. As part of the program the students attend the National Convention of the National Federation of the Blind. In this photo the student is making her way around the convention, gaining skills and confidence while being mentored by the man with the cane.

Learning to move at a convention and rely on travel skills is very empowering to develop confidence in independent movement and travel. Such mentoring opportunities where the blind learn from the blind afford the student unlimited possibilities to learn the skills of blindness. Mentoring possibilities offered by the organized blind are listed in the Resources chapter.

66. Blind Travel Instructor and His Student

Description: These last two photos were taken in Ruston, Louisiana, the home of the Louisiana Center for the Blind. In this photo Harold Wilson, instructing independent movement and travel, is working with his student crossing a street. The level and kind of monitoring would depend on the skills the student is learning, as in any student-teacher relationship.

Blind professional service providers role model the skills of blindness for their students in a way that sighted instructors can not. There are some sighted instructors who use sleep shades on themselves to teach their students. In this case, they too would role model the nonvisual travel skills. Information regarding blind persons teaching independent movement and travel is presented in the Resources chapter.

67. Instruction Under Sleep Shades

Description: Blind instructors make the best mentors and role models for the blind student. My first lesson under sleep shades was with Arlene Hill, an instructor of the Louisiana Center for the Blind. She is pictured here with one of her students.

Learning some cane and orientation skills under sleep shades with Arlene was a positive experience for me. There was an attunement in our interactions that made the lesson valuable and useful. Learning under sleep shades is discussed as one of the building blocks in chapter 1 and for partially sighted children in chapter 3.

For the reader new to O&M I hope this chapter has offered vivid examples of *independent movement and travel and the process toward independence*. For the reader trained in conventional O&M, such as I was, it is my hope that this chapter has fueled your motivation to expand your beliefs, attitudes and practices. For the reader who has worked with blind children from the bottom-up and sought alternative ways of approaching independent movement and travel, I hope this chapter has offered you new ideas for your work with blind children.

By the way, if you haven't noticed, a photo of the most prevalent skill taught to blind children in conventional O&M is absent. Let me explain why. The sighted/human guide is the most well known mobility technique used for and by blind children. There have been more photos with detailed explanations of this guided technique than any other in the conventional O&M publications, therefore, readers will be familiar with it. From the Promotion Model point of view, it is the last skill to be emphasized for the independent movement and travel of blind children. Therefore, its absence among the photos is a way of making a statement about the lack of priority given to this skill. It doesn't mean it can't or shouldn't be used; rather, it simply means that the Promotion Model does not place an emphasis on this method of travel. And lastly, the sighted/human guide technique is a skill for the one who is doing the guiding and not for the blind child.

In this book there are photos of about 30 different blind children. Seventy percent of these children have developmental delays other than blindness, ranging from mild to severe. Some of the reasons for the delays were severe premature birth, additional sensory losses, cerebral palsy, emotional disturbances, autism, and cognitive impairments. I have intentionally avoided labeling the additional disability unless it was absolutely necessary.

Instead, I have chosen to integrate them into this developmental guide with the appropriate alternative skills. I have done this for the simple reason that many of the suggestions may be useful for *all* blind children, depending on their developmental level. For example, Active Learning is beneficial to all children and not only to multiple disabled blind children. I have also avoided assigning chronological ages to the photos because I wanted to focus on the developmental level and the alternative skill being offered. The validity of the alternative approach, as chronicled in these photos, can be applied to the blind child at any age/stage appropriate developmental level. It is the child's developmental needs that determine the skill to be learned. This is not to say that we should not expect the child to be age appropriate but that some children may not be able to be age appropriate. Such developmentally delayed children can learn to be stage developmentally appropriate in skill acquisition and skill proficiency if we offer them a "menu" of experiences that *will* work for them.

Among the 30% of children in these photos who do not have developmental delays, some of them are advanced for their age, using the "norms" for normal child development. Just as sight has nothing to do with the advanced development of a sighted child, blindness has nothing to do with the advanced development of a blind child. Sight or blindness does not cause advancement or delays in development. Blindness is simply a characteristic of the child. The Promotion Model factors in this characteristic and offers alternative approaches and solutions that foster development and independence in children.

What matters is the opportunity to learn in a way that promotes independent movement and travel in blind children. As adults, we are called upon to develop a continuum of learning that connects *to all children and treats all children with respect for who they are and what they need to become independent in movement and travel.*

CHAPTER 6

INDEPENDENT MOVEMENT AND TRAVEL FOR A NEW MILLENNIUM

At the Louisiana Tech University O&M program students,
as well as staff, are blind and sighted.

Independent Movement and Travel in Blind Children: A Promotion Model, pp. 305–319
Copyright © 2007 by Information Age Publishing
305

> *We owe children the best that humankind has to offer.*
> —United Nations Declaration

As a sighted individual, I was trained in the conventional approach of orientation and mobility (O&M), which was developed by sighted individuals working within an adult-centered rehabilitation service delivery system. The foundation for the coursework I took to become a certified teacher of the blind and to be certified in New Jersey to teach O&M was developed decades earlier, prior to 1970. As professional service providers our knowledge was based on *what we thought we knew about the development of sighted children and blind children* at that time. In addition, the blind adults who learned "formalized" O&M were once sighted individuals who had lost vision in World War II. Therefore, our information that guided us to teach O&M at that time was based on a sighted person's point of view of what the curriculum would be to teach blind adults to become independent travelers.

During the same time that the protocols were being developed by sighted individuals to teach O&M, blind consumers were beginning to organize around the country and develop their own perspectives of independent movement and travel. The organized blind of post World War II were not invited to be partners in developing the core curriculum of what was to become the foundation for the O&M profession. In addition, at that time the input of parents of blind children was not a consideration. And lastly, the last decades of the twentieth century gave us new research and insights regarding how babies and preschool children learn. Therefore, the university preparatory programs in O&M that would subsequently develop by the 1960s did so without the input of the organized blind, parents of blind children, and what we would come to know about early child development.

It is not surprising then that the curriculum developed post World War II would dominate the field in the later half of the twentieth century and would need to be altered to reflect the point of view of those not included in the original design of conventional O&M.

This book gives testimony and chronicles an alternative approach based upon partnerships with the organized blind and parents of blind children for the independent movement and travel of blind children. The Promotion Model is the tip of the iceberg of what *we can come to know* to advance the independent movement and travel of blind children. In 35 years of teaching blind children I have learned to select from my conventional training what has worked and eliminate what has not been effective to promote independent movement and travel. The result is the Promotion Model with its building blocks that respect the developmental progressions of the child.

The contents of this book are the result of partnerships with the parents of blind children, the organized blind, and a variety of professional service providers both in the field of blindness and generic early childhood education. It has been my experience that the results of these partnerships translate goals and objectives into reliable and effective practices that produce successful outcomes in children. Such worthwhile partnerships need to be promoted, nurtured, and expanded if we are to offer our best to blind children in the twenty-first century.

PARTNERSHIPS PROMOTE INDEPENDENCE IN BLIND CHILDREN

In the last quarter of the twentieth century there emerged an increasing awareness of the need for positive early intervention in the education of all children. This new emphasis on early learning had an effect on our interest in blind children to develop their independent movement and travel capabilities in their early intervention and preschool years. It was only a matter of time that successful child-centered philosophies and practices evolved as an alternative to the conventional O&M approaches. We would come to learn that the story about the blind child is not one of vision loss and deficit-thinking about blindness but of developmental gains that the child will make and the positive thinking of alternative, nonvisual skills for the child to learn. The age of enlightenment regarding the independent movement and travel of blind children had begun.

Our enlightenment is part of a worldwide educational revolution that questions our deficit-thinking about the disabilities of children and how they learn and replaces such an approach with asset-oriented thinking about the potentialities and possibilities each child has for learning. For instance, Dr. Lilli Nielsen's Active Learning, designed for the multiple disabled blind child, has had an impact on the education of all blind children and for other multiple disabled children who are not blind. Another example is Conductive Education out of Hungary. The emphasis on functional daily living skills is clearly defined in its programming for children that have a variety of disabilities—motor, sensory, and cognitive. Like Active Learning, Conductive Education promotes the active movement and life skills development of children. When an educational philosophy is sound and reliable it crosses over into the mainstream education of all children.

In this country the development of an alternative philosophy and educational practices to the conventional approach in O&M for blind children is building momentum, as we have turned the corner into the twenty-first century. Practitioners of O&M and other blindness professionals who have worked with blind children from the bottom-up have had the opportunities to learn about the positive impact of appropriate early intervention practices with children. Increasingly, conventionally trained professional service providers have altered their perspectives and practices and developed partnerships with the organized blind to promote the independent movement and travel of blind children.

The organized blind have more than challenged the outdated practices that are part of the conventional approach to teach blind children. They have offered alternatives, and guidance as well, to promote the independence of all blind persons. As a conventionally trained service provider, I believe that I was able to develop the Promotion Model because of the partnerships I made with the organized blind. As a sighted O&M professional I welcomed the opportunity to learn from skilled blind persons and the parents of blind children who partner with them.

Unfortunately, many professional service providers in the field of blindness have not embraced the opportunity to partner with the organized blind, attend their seminars or conventions and learn about new philosophy and approaches to educating blind children. The organized blind are building momentum in the offering of programs and opportunities for professional service providers to learn new perspectives and practices that will benefit blind children. More than ever before, the possibility for partnerships between parents, professional service providers, and the organized blind exist to facilitate the independent movement and travel in blind children.

The potential that blind children bring into this world is no guarantee that their innate need to know and drive to move will be expressed and offers no assurance that their abilities will be developed *without* the opportunities to learn and achieve. We professional service providers have our goals and service delivery plan for blind children. Some of these services are well intended but they are built on concepts of outdated thinking and not necessarily built on the reliable actions of people. *Concepts don't act, people do!*

We are more likely to act on what we know when we truly believe in the outcome, as in the independent movement and travel in blind children. We are more likely to promote independence for blind children when parents, professional service providers, and the organized blind are involved in the beliefs, concepts and practices that drive our actions with blind children,. We are more likely to be successful in our collective actions through effective partnerships.

It is interesting to observe how the need for information about blindness develops through partnerships that occur in grade school with sighted and blind children. For example, when I was teaching O&M within elementary schools I would often give a little talk to the sighted children in the class, along with the blind child and sometimes the parent of the blind child. We would start off by asking these children what they thought about "blindness." Over the years I've kept a list of their responses. Here are a few:

- I don't like to think about blindness because it is so sad.
- How do they know what to do?
- What if their dog bites them?
- We should take care of blind people.
- How do they brush their teeth?
- They must crash a lot.
- Blind people make me think of deaf people.
- How do they decorate for the holidays?

These are candid responses from children who are beginning to learn about blindness from their blind classmate. After the blind child, parent and I would talk and demonstrate some of the skills of blindness—writing Braille, reading a Braille watch and using a cane—we would ask the children to draw a picture of what they learned and one sentence to describe their drawing. The responses were often so precious and refreshingly spontaneous. For example, they would draw some of the following:

- First a blind child bumping into a wall without a cane and then using a cane to stop before the wall. The caption: I do not feel an "ouch."
- A picture of a Braille book and the blind child reading it. The caption: This is a dot book.
- A blind child listening to a wall with radio waves coming out of his ear. The caption: They listen with their ears and try real hard with their senses.
- A blind child finding the edge of a step with a cane. The caption: The blind child sees with the cane.

The *attitudinal change* these children can undergo in one half-hour of "show and tell" lifts the human spirit. The sighted children enjoy learning about Braille and the cane from the blind child. They learn from the parent of the blind child too. The blind child also learns from sighted peers about what it means to live in a sighted world and about the alternative skills needed to interact, make friends, and achieve. These are partnerships developed from the bottom-up in the lives of young blind and sighted children. We adults can take an example from the children in the development of partnerships, especially if we have not sought partnerships out or, when given the opportunity, did not embrace them.

Parents of young blind children benefit greatly from partnerships with professional service providers and skilled blind persons who can mentor them and their child. Blind children need instruction and practice in the skills leading to independent movement and travel. The blind child is more likely to develop the age/stage appropriate skills for independence when the collective actions of partnerships work toward a common goal.

PARTNERSHIPS INCREASE OUR RESOURCES FOR BLIND CHILDREN

As we move further into the twenty-first century, an additional challenge to promoting independent movement and travel in blind children is the shortage of personnel to service the needs of blind children. O&M specialists who work in state agencies, large school districts, or who cover large rural areas, for example, know the shortages of instructors and the forever increasing caseloads. I was one such instructor responsible for seeing as many as 100 blind people in 1 year. How could I possibly have met the O&M needs of all these individuals? How often does our role as O&M specialist become reduced to consulting, minimal evaluation, and hardly any teaching under these circumstances? The multiplicity of these children's needs at home and school threatened me with burn out and limited opportunities for professional growth. I learned that partnering with parents and the organized blind enabled me to survive the "blindness system."

We—the parents of blind children, professional service providers, particularly the O&M specialists and the organized blind—all share in the challenge to meet the independent movement and travel needs of blind children. We can do this! Together, we can change the blindness system. It is the new millennium and a new time for change. We have little to fear in working together. In creating new change, we are all beginners and recognize our interdependence on one another.

Partnership among parents, professional service providers and the organized blind can strengthen and increase our resources. Below are a several examples of how we can do this.

Alternative Certifications

We can increase the number of O&M specialists working with blind children by recognizing and utilizing *alternative* certifications. Many travel instructors, sighted and blind, who do not meet conventional O&M criteria to teach independent movement and travel to blind children, could meet alternative criteria for certification already established. These experienced and qualified individuals are an underutilized workforce. Why is this so? One reason is the resistance of employers of O&M professionals to consider alternative certifications other than the one provided by the conventional O&M profession. These school districts and private and public agencies for the blind limit themselves to the conventional O&M certification. This is so because the conventional O&M professional organizations promote negative attitudes and lack an accurate understanding of the certification alternatives that are available. If we are to truly embrace partnerships, the professional organizations of conventional O&M must come to value and promote alternatives. *The ultimate goal of employment of professionals in the blindness system is not to promote the agenda of the professional's needs, but to advance the cause and meet the needs of blind people.*

In the 29th Institute on Rehabilitation Issues publication *Contemporary Issues in Orientation and Mobility,* qualifications for O&M instructors are discussed as well as alternative certification possibilities. See the Resources chapter for this publication.

Role Releasing to Parents, School Staff, and Teachers of the Blind

We can role release by teaching our skills to parents and school staff and by demystifying O&M and making it the most natural and easy thing for the blind child to learn in the early years. By respecting the parent as the blind child's first O&M teacher, we can have a partner in sharing the responsibility for instructing independent movement and travel. By communicating and training parents we create a larger community of "teachers" in O&M.

Additionally, there are teachers of the blind who, because they are not dual certified in O&M, do not address the child's O&M needs. The O&M profession can promote the positive thinking by teachers of the blind to become more involved in the independent movement and travel of children when no O&M professional is available. When there is not an O&M specialist available, teachers of the blind should be addressing the early movement and travel needs of blind children and promoting the use of the cane. In the college preparatory programs for teachers of the blind, the students take a basic course in O&M. This course and their experience with blind children make them the next best professional service provider to promote independent movement and travel.

Any teacher of the blind can promote such basic movement and travel skills without adversely reducing instruction time with the blind child to learn other skills. When basic training in independent movement and travel and the cane is offered to parents and the school staff by the teacher of the blind, the responsibility of various adults is shared and the child can practice skills in the natural environments of home and school.

Utilizing Early Intervention and Preschool Staff to Facilitate Independent Movement and Travel

Early intervention and preschool professionals are knowledgeable about early child development and the developmental delays of children. These professionals welcome information about blindness to facilitate the intervention of the blind children in their programs. For example, physical and occupational therapists are very creative when incorporating information about active movement and the use of the cane into their therapy time with blind children. But what if an O&M professional or other blindness professional is not available to share information about independent movement and travel of blind children?

I suggest that there should be a concerted effort on the part of the organized blind and professional service providers to share O&M information with early intervention and preschool professionals. This can be done by sharing information at the variety of venues attended by these professionals for their professional growth. I am not suggesting, for example, that a physical or occupational therapist by attending a training session can provide a thorough program in O&M for a blind child. But I am suggesting that in the absence of an O&M service provider, a physical or occupational therapist can be very instrumental in introducing basic independent movement and travel experiences to the blind children. This would include introducing the young blind child how to use the cane to move in the world. After all, physical and occupational therapists utilize a variety of alternative mobility devices in their practice. The cane would simply be one more alternative device. Such therapists partnering with parents can facilitate and promote age/stage appropriate independent movement and travel.

Respect for the Organized Blind

We can and should expect from professional service providers, particularly from the specialty of O&M, an across the board respect for the organized blind and for the requirements that the blind have set forth in their mission for equality, opportunity, and security. This respect for partnership with the organized blind by professionals would benefit the independence of blind children. For example, the National Federation of the Blind, the National Organization of Parents of Blind Children, and the Jernigan Institute are providers of clear, reliable, and useful information about blindness. These consumers are also professional service providers who will strengthen our resources and increase our agreed upon knowledge to promote independent movement and travel in blind children.

This also means respect for the nonconventional preparatory programs for teachers of blind students and O&M at Louisiana Tech University. Louisiana Tech's O&M program promotes an alternative curriculum to conventional O&M. Their students are blind and sighted, so sleep shades are used regardless of the vision proficiency of the students preparing to be O&M professionals. Because vision is not considered essential to teach O&M, coursework stresses the nonvisual skills of blindness. Unlike the conventional approach to O&M that begins with the sighted/human guide, the Louisiana Tech O&M program presents this method of travel at the end of the curriculum, preferring instead to start off with the instruction in the use of the cane.

Graduates of this program are encouraged to work with consumers and the organized blind. Partnerships with consumers are seen as part of the solution of meeting the needs of blind persons for independent movement and travel, and not as part of the problem. For more information about these programs check with the Professional Development and Research Institute on Blindness listed in the Resources section.

THE BEST WE HAVE TO OFFER

The Promotion Model is a blueprint for the independent movement and travel of blind children. By combining our efforts we can work together to develop a more detailed, developmental continuum of alternative skills from the bottom-up for blind children. The spectrum of alternative, nonvisual skills would represent a continuity of strategies and practices addressing the infant blind child to adult development of the skills of blindness.

The result would be a comprehensive, developmental O&M assessment and guide for early intervention and preschool years that promotes the independent movement and travel of blind children. This would include the introduction to cane travel without the necessity for a precane for blind children.

Incorporating Reliable and Useful Coursework in Infant Studies (Birth to 3) and Preschool (3 to 5) Years Into the O&M Curriculum

Coursework preparing O&M professionals must be up to date about "normal" child development. This means educating the student preparing to be an O&M professional about the development of babies, birth to 3 years of age. This also means educating students about the development of the child during the preschool years. Once students have a more thorough understanding of normal development and the impact of the child's movement on development in the early years, then the alternative approaches for the blind child can be more clearly understood and promoted. This coursework would be very useful for O&M professionals to more confidently approach the blind baby and blind preschool child, with or without developmental delays.

Over the years I have talked with a number of directors of conventional O&M programs throughout the country and they believe that they have an early childhood component to their O&M program. What matters, however, isn't that there are courses in their preparatory programs but that the content of these courses are accurate, reliable, and useful to their students. I respectfully suggest that if the coursework was reliable, the students graduating from such programs would be more comfortable working with the younger blind population. These students would be confident in their understanding of the development needs of these children and teach practices that promote independent movement and travel in blind children at an age/stage appropriate time.

My observations of and conversations with these graduates indicates an uneasy feeling about teaching this early childhood population of blind children, an inadequate understanding of typical child development and consequently, an unintended delaying of promoting independent movement and travel.

Coursework regarding infants and preschool children that relate to the O&M practitioner would best be devised and coordinated by a partnership effort. Such a partnership would use the best infant and preschool studies departments around the country. The organized blind, parents of blind children, organizations and O&M professionals in the field who are comfortable, confident, and effective in working with these young blind children to produce independent movement and travel outcomes would form the foundation of such a partnership. Therefore, the coursework would be the best we have to offer.

Offering our Best in the New Millennium

The ultimate goal is to create a partnership, working together to facilitate the highest level of achievement for blind children. Working together we can come to promote the independent movement and travel of blind children. In the words of Dietrich Bonhoeffer we will come to understand that "there are things for which an uncompromising stand is worthwhile." This book has presented an uncompromising stand in presenting the Promotion Model as an alternative to conventional O&M.

The problem is not the blind children or how the children learn independent movement and travel skills. The problem comes when we teach them: will we work together to give them the best we have to offer? Above all else we must first "do no harm" to the children. The children are ready, willing, and waiting to learn. It is our beliefs, attitudes, and expectations that can open or close doors for them. If we are cautious with our assumptions about blindness and if we work confidently together on what we know works best, then the years ahead in this millennium will be years of options, opportunities, and growth toward independence for blind children.

RESOURCES

The resources below include organizations, programs, publications, videos, and materials that offer positive, useful, and reliable information about blindness, typical development in sighted children, and/or blind children, and promote independent movement and travel.

National Federation of the Blind
1800 Johnson Street
Baltimore, MD 21230
Telephone: 410-659-9314
Email: nfb@nfb.org
Web site: www.nfb.org

The National Federation of the Blind (NFB) is an organization of blind people, families, and friends working toward the equality, opportunity, and security for the blind. This organization provides information, literature, educational materials and training.

A variety of aids and appliances, literature, and videos can be ordered through their Materials Center, including *the NFB type cane* discussed in chapter 4 (lightweight, fiberglass, or carbon fiber with a metal tip) and the following publications:

Independent Movement and Travel in Blind Children: A Promotion Model, pp. 321–330
Copyright © 2007 by Information Age Publishing

- *Braille Monitor*, the NFB's monthly publication, offers consumer-driven information that deals with a variety of topics of interest and concerns to blind persons of all ages.
- *Modular Instruction for Independent Travel for Students who are Blind or Visually Impaired: Preschool through High School*, Willoughby, Doris M. and Monthei, Sharon L, NFB, 1998.
- *Techniques Used by Blind Cane Travel Instructors*, Maria Morais, Paul Lorensen, Roland Allen, Edward C. Bell, Arlene Hill, and Eric Woods, NFB, 1997.
- *Care and Feeding of the Long White Cane: Instructions in Cane Travel for Blind People*, Thomas Bickford, NFB, 1993.
- The Kernel Book Series, NFB. A series of books with personal stories written about and by blind people.
- *Julie and Brandon: Our Blind Friends* is an activity and coloring book for children to understand some of the skills of blindness blind children will use in school.

National Organization of Parents of Blind Children
1800 Johnson Street
Baltimore, MD 21230
Telephone: 410-659-9314
Email: bcheadle@nfb.org
Web site: www.nfb.org/nopbc.htm

The National Organization of Parents of Blind Children (NOPBC) is an organization of parents of blind children, teachers, and friends working to promote opportunities for blind children at home, school, and community. They provide positive role models for parents of blind children as well as training, resources, information, and support.

They publish the magazine *Future Reflections* for parents and teachers. The *Special Issue-The Early Years*, Volume 23,

Number 2 has many outstanding articles written for this early childhood population.

Videos are available that offer guidance on orientation and mobility with blind children. Two particularly valuable videos are:

- *White Canes for Blind Kids*, NFB produced on VHS. 12 minutes. This video demonstrates how the use of the long white cane can transform the lives of blind children. Through interviews with parents and scenes of young people—from toddlers to teens—learning to get around with the long cane. Footage of this video was taken at a National Convention of the National Federation of the Blind.
- *Avoiding IEP Disasters,* NFB produced, six-part series containing a total of over 2 and a half hours of information. Part Six is titled: "Perspectives from a Teacher of the Blind and Visually Impaired and an Orientation and Mobility Specialist" (29 minutes). Videos can be purchased individually or the entire series.

**The Jernigan Institute of the
National Federation of the Blind**
1800 Johnson Street
Baltimore, MD 21230
Telephone: 410-659-9314
Email: MRiccobono@nfb.org
Web site: www.nfb.org/nfbji/enter.htm

Among its many goals, the Jernigan Institute offers educational opportunities for blind youth with early intervention initiatives. Programs, services, research, and technology reflect the consumer perspective. For information regarding education programs contact Mark A. Riccobono, director of education of the Jernigan Institute.

Blind Children's Resource Center
Parents of Blind Children-NJ
23 Alexander Ave.
Madison, NJ 07940
Telephone: 973-625-5999
Email: center@webspan.net
Web site: www.blindchildren.org

This Web site features information about blindness/ visual impairment, education and child development, independent movement and travel, physical education, and "making it work" in the regular school. Some of my information about promoting independence in blind children's orientation and mobility can be found here.

The LEAD Program
Telephone: 866-632-1940

LEAD (Leadership, Education, Advocacy and Determination) is a mentoring program for blind teenagers developed by Joe Ruffalo, the president of the National Federation of the Blind of New Jersey. Blind mentors meet on weekends with blind teenagers to positively role model how to be full participants in society.

Education of the Blind Child
A very useful and reliable guide for promoting success in the regular school for the blind child is *Making it Work: Educating the Blind/Visually Impaired Student in the Regular School,* by Carol Castellano, Information Age Publishing, Charlotte, North Carolina, 2005 (www.infoagepub.com). This book is also available on CD.

Books on Early Childhood Development

The following books provide useful information on parenting practices, infant development and behavior in "typical" development in the sighted baby and/or offering developmental guidance for the blind baby.

- *The Baby Book: Everything you need to know about your baby from birth to age two.* William Sears, MD, and Martha Sears, RN, 1992, 2003; Little Brown and Company, 1271 Ave. of the Americas, New York, NY, 10020.
- *The First Three Years of Life.* Burton L. White, 1990 Burton L. White Associates, Inc., Prentice Hall Press, 15 Columbus Circle, NY 10023.
- *Your Baby and Child from Birth to Age Five.* Penelope Leach, Alfred A. Knopf, New York, 6th edition, 1992.
- *Show Me What My Friends Can See.* Patricia Sonksen, and Blanche Stiff, 1991. From the Institute on Child Heath, London WC1N1EH. Order by writing to 'Developmental Guide', The Wolfson Centre, Mecklenburg Square, London, WCIN 2AP. Fax: 071-833-9469.
- *A Parent's Guide to Understanding Sensory Integration, 1986,* Sensory Integration International, 1402 Cravens Ave., Torrence, CA 90501, Telephone: (213) 533-8338.
- *Pathways to Independence: Orientation and Mobility Skills for Your Infant and Toddler,* Barbara O'Mara, 1989. Order by writing or calling the Lighthouse, National Center for Vision and Child Development, 111 East 59th Street, New York, NY 10022, 212-355-2200.

Children With Additional Disabilities

Vision Associates
2109 West US HWY 90 Suite 170 #312
Lake City, FL 32055
Telephone: 407-352-1200
Email: Website@visionkits.com
Web site: www.visionkits.com

"Lilli Books"
Lilli Books
Drejensvej 86
DK 6000 Kolding
Denmark
Telephone: 45 75 51 57 65
Email: lillibooks@mail.dk
Web site: www.lillibooks.com

Lilli Books is a company publishing and distributing books written by Dr. Lilli Nielsen and Dr. Van der Pool. The company sells the books, available in both Danish and English, in most of the world, specializing in the "especially developmentally threatened child" with multiple disabilities. Books that are very useful in promoting movement in babies and multiply impaired children (developmentally under four years of age) include: *Early Learning- Step by Step* (2001); *Are You Blind?* (2003); *The Comprehending Hand* (1994); *FIELA Curriculum; and Space and Self* (2003).

LilliWorks Active Learning Foundation
1815 Encinal Avenue
Alameda, CA 94501
Telephone: 510-814-9111
Email: info@lilliworks.com
Web site: www.lilliworks.org

LilliWorks Active Learning Foundation is the exclusive authorized provider of Dr. Nielsen-designed Active Learning equipment. Their mission is to provide optimal Active Learning environments to the children that can benefit from them, and to support Active Learning with education, training, outreach, research and development.

Penrickton Center for Blind Children
Patricia Obrzut, M.S., O.T.R.
26530 Eureka Road
Taylor, MI 48180
Telephone: 734-946-7500
Email: patty@penrickton.com
Web site: www.penrickton.com

The Penrickton Center for Blind Children offers a variety of services for the blind, multiple disabled child between the ages of 1-12: a 5-day residential educational program, day care, consultation, and evaluation. This program has all of the equipment developed by Dr. Nielsen for Active Learning.

Conductive Education
National Institute for Conductive Education
Russell Rd, Birmingham
B138RD
Telephone: 0121 449 1569
Email: info@conductive-education.org.uk
Web site: www.conductive-education.org.uk

Conductive Education is a program that originated from Hungary, designed for the education of disabled children. Its philosophy promotes the independent movement of the child. There are various web sites that offer information about conductive education, its philosophy and educational materials.

The National Information Clearinghouse on Children Who Are Deaf-Blind
DB-Link
345 No. Monmouth Ave.
Monmouth, OR 97361
Telephone: 1-800-438-9376
E-mail: dblink@tr.wou.edu
Web site: www.tr.wou.edu/dblink

The National Information Clearinghouse on Children Who Are Deaf-Blind offers information to nurture, empower, and instruct children who are deaf-blind, including national and state resource sheets.

Textbook on Travel in the Deaf-Blind

A textbook that is particularly useful in working with older blind children and adults is *Independence Without Sight or Sound, Suggestions for Practitioners Working with Deaf/Blind Adults*, Dona Sauerburger, 1993, American Foundation for the Blind, 15 West, 16th St., New York, NY, 10011

Publications on the Nonconventional Approaches to Orientation and Mobility and Empowerment of the Blind

- *Cognitive Learning Theory and Cane Travel: a New Paradigm*, Dr. Richard Mettler, 1995. Order by writing Rehabilitation Services for the Visually Impaired, 4600 Valley Rd., Lincoln, Nebraska 68510-4844. Telephone: 402-471-2891.

- *Contemporary Issues in Orientation and Mobility*, 29th Institute on Rehabilitation Issues, 2004, published by U.S. Department of Education granted through George Washington University, Regional Continuing Education Program, 2011 Eye Street, NW, Suite 300, Washington, DC 20052.
- *Freedom for the Blind: The Secret is Empowerment*, James H. Omvig, Region VI Rehabilitation Continuing Education Program, University of Arkansas, 2002.
- *We Know Who We Are: A History of the Blind in Challenging Educational and Socially Constructed Policies, A Study in Policy Archeology*, Ronald J. Ferguson, 2002, by Caddo Gap Press, 3145 Geary Boulevard PMB 275, San Francisco, CA 94118.
- *The Blindness Revolution:* Jernigan in his own words, by James H. Omvig, 2005, Information Age Publishing, Charlotte, NC, www.infoagepub.com.
- *Education and Rehabilitation for Empowerment*, Ed Vaughan and James M. Omvig, 2005, Information Age Publishing, Charlotte, NC, www.infoagepub .com.

Professional Development and Research Institute on Blindness

Dr. Edward Bell, Director
Or Dr. Ruby Ryles
Professional Development and Research Institute on Blindness
Louisiana Tech University
P.O. Box 3158
Ruston, LA 71272
Telephone: 318-257-4554

E-mail: instituteonblindness@latech.edu
Web site: www.instituteonblindness.latech.edu

The Professional Development and Research Institute on Blindness is a department in the College of Education at Louisiana Tech University and is a joint venture between the University and the Louisiana Center for the Blind. The purpose of the Institute is to provide leadership in creating programs and conducting research that recognizes the socially constructed assumptions underpinning the current structure of the blindness system and research being done on blindness. Their O&M program utilizes Structured Discovery Learning and they offer certification in Teaching Blind Students, which emphasizes high expectations and Braille literacy.

ABOUT THE AUTHOR

Joseph Cutter has more than 35 years experience as an O&M specialist and teacher of the blind. A pioneer in the area of developmental O&M, he created New Jersey's Early Childhood O&M program in 1974. His child-centered, team approach applies the alternative skills of blindness in order to promote independent movement and travel in blind children. In 1994 Mr. Cutter received the Distinguished Educator of Blind Children Award from the National Federation of the Blind. In 2006, at the National Convention of the National Federation of the Blind, Mr. Cutter received the Fredric K. Schroeder Award for Orientation and Mobility from the National Blindness Professional Certification Board. Today he is retired from state service and is a sought-after speaker, seminar leader, and consultant in early childhood O&M.

Printed in the United States
91017LV00001B/118/A

9 781593 116033